ENGLAND AS YOU LIKE IT

An Independent Traveler's Companion

Susan Allen Toth

BALLANTINE BOOKS • NEW YORK

Some of these chapters originally appeared, under different titles
and in slightly different form, in the *New York Times*, *Washington Post*,
Minneapolis *Star Tribune*, and *Victoria*.

Library of Congress Catalog Card Number: 95-95004

ISBN: 0-345-40190-5

Cover design by Susan Grube
Cover painting by Mark Strathy

Manufactured in the United States of America

First Trade Paperback Edition: March 1996

10 9 8 7 6 5 4 3 2 1

For James, who is always eager to try the next footpath,

AND

for those who have shared with me their own love of England

Contents

INTRODUCTION

A Note to Readers on What's Ahead   3
Catching Hold of "A Few Floating Facts"   6

I. FOLLOWING YOUR OWN FOOTPATH

1   How to Be Your Own Travel Agent   9
2   Draw Me a Map!   54
3   First-Class Illusion: Traveling Coach   61
4   The Joys of Eating In   67
5   In Praise of Overpacking   72
6   A Supermarket of Souvenirs   77
7   How to Keep a Travel Journal   84

II. THE THUMBPRINT THEORY OF TRAVEL

A Note on the Thumbprint Theory of Travel   97
8   A Spyglass on Padstow Harbor   99
9   Hidden Corners in Du Maurier Country   110

10 Dorset Days   *121*
    Yes, I Know Scotland Is Not England:
      An Explanatory Note   *132*
11 Gentle Walks in the Wild Highlands   *134*
12 Quiet Surprises in the Northeast Highlands   *144*

III. SPECIAL PLACES

    A Note on Special Places   *157*
13 St. Michael's Mount: A Fairy-Tale Castle   *159*
14 Ashdown Forest: Pooh Country   *168*
15 Lord of the Manor: Staying at Standen   *179*
16 Lynmouth: Savoring an English Honey Pot   *189*
17 Two Scottish War Memorials   *198*
18 Secret Gardens of the City of London   *204*
19 London's National Postal Museum   *216*
20 Bluebell Woods   *223*
    Planning the Next Trip?   *232*
    Index   *235*

Introduction

A Note to Readers on What's Ahead

"What are some of your favorite places in England?" "How did you find them?" "What kind of travel agent do you use?" "How do you decide where to stay?" "Can you share any of your travel secrets?" Soon after the publication of my first book about England, *My Love Affair with England: A Traveler's Memoir*, I found myself trying to answer these and many other specific questions. Some of my readers had already traveled to England at least once and were now ready to plan a different trip. Others hoped to go for the first time and wanted to be sure they used their time wisely.

Talking to these new friends or reading their letters, often filled with their own nostalgic, funny, or bittersweet memories of England, I also sensed that most Americans traveling abroad are concerned, as I am, about expenses. Although my husband James and I do splurge occasionally on a fancy hotel or elegant dinner, I try to plan our trips very carefully so that we stay within a reasonable budget. Otherwise we could not travel to England as often as we do.

Traveling independently in England—avoiding package

tours and making most plans and arrangements on my own—
is probably my most fundamental "travel secret." To discover
the England of his or her dreams, a traveler has to be able to
follow individual tastes, inclinations, and intuitions. To keep
expenses low, the independent traveler can often search out alternatives that would take too long to find, or require too
much detailed knowledge, for most travel agents. And, as I
point out in Chapter One, How to Be Your Own Travel
Agent, why should *they* have all the fun?

England As You Like It is the record of one woman's independent travel in England, written in the hope that it will inspire,
encourage, and inform others on their own idiosyncratic journeys. Idiosyncratic does not necessarily mean cycling along the
edge of a cliff, or jumping on and off trains at a moment's whim,
or arriving in Bath at midnight without a place to stay. I like to
read about trips like that, but I don't like to take them. I admit I
prefer to be reasonably comfortable when I travel.

I am not an easy, carefree traveler. I worry a lot, I am always sure everything will go wrong, and I am always amazed
when it (almost always) doesn't. So following my itineraries
will not lead anyone into desperate situations—neither plunged
knee-deep into an Exmoor bog nor jostled in a mile-long line
to see the Crown Jewels at the Tower. My suggestions are always seasoned by experience and caution, with a substantial
dash of adventure and a huge dollop of curiosity.

Times and places change, and no one will duplicate (or
want to!) every detail of my own travels. Perhaps the ice
cream stand near the shopping precinct in Lynmouth will
have closed—but Lynmouth, with its small fishing pier, seaside and riverside walks, and brooding cliffs, will still be there.
If you find yourself at St. Michael's Mount in the middle of a

sunny August afternoon, you may not enjoy an entirely peaceful and solitary stay. But the view from the parapets will still be breathtaking, and you can let the tour groups sweep by as you gaze over sail-dotted Mount's Bay.

For the understandable—and often compelling—reasons of time, convenience, and security, some travelers, of course, will always prefer to sign onto an organized tour. For them, I hope this guide will give an added depth and perspective to their experience. Tucking an Ordnance Survey map in your tote bag, for example (see Chapter Two, Draw Me a Map!), might make a long day on a bus (or *coach* as the English would say) not only seem much shorter but more interesting. If you feel embarrassed at how much luggage you're carrying, take comfort from Chapter Five, In Praise of Overpacking.

At the end of one friendly, query-packed letter, another lover of England wrote me: "If you ever find yourself having to make a trip alone to England, and you need a companion, please get in touch with me. I'd love to travel the way you do." She meant, I think, that she'd like to go to some special places, discover a few on her own, and feel confident—even exuberant—while exploring the varied pleasures of England. This guide, disguised as a collection of travel essays, is intended to help and encourage her.

In the first section, Following Your Own Footpath, I offer some general travel tips, from how to plan a trip—itinerary, hotels, rental cottages, cars—to how to shop for inexpensive souvenirs. In the second section, The Thumbprint Theory of Travel, I provide five specific examples of how to spend a rewarding week based in a small village or in the countryside. The third section, Special Places, describes some of my favorite destinations.

Readers of *My Love Affair with England* will recognize in these pages the familiar figure of "James," who is, of course, James Stageberg, my husband, roving architect, chauffeur, associate chef, and fellow explorer of footpaths.

CATCHING HOLD OF "A FEW FLOATING FACTS": A CAUTIONARY NOTE TO READERS

Where it seems relevant, I have added a brief section called "A Few Floating Facts" at the end of certain chapters. In this section, I give some specific names, phone numbers, and, if possible, fax numbers, for rental agencies, tourist boards, hotels, restaurants, and further sources of information.

I call this section "A Few Floating Facts" to remind readers that these facts are subject to change—just as currency is said to *float*, depending on the vagaries of the international monetary market. A restaurant may go out of business, a discount program may change its rules, the price of a weekly rental may increase with inflation. As a general rule, prices always bob up—never down.

Not long ago, when I was in New York with only an hour to spare, I dashed to an address I had taken from a current guidebook for the British Tourist Authority, then located on West 57th Street—or so I thought. When I arrived, I found an Italian restaurant. Only after frantically searching for a phone booth and calling the B.T.A. did I discover it had just moved to Fifth Avenue.

So be gently warned: my facts were right at the time of going to press, but facts do float. Check to make sure the mooring is still there before you set sail.

I

Following Your Own Footpath

1

How to Be Your Own Travel Agent

This chapter deals with the nitty-gritty details of how I plan our trips to England, from choosing our itinerary to finding accommodations to selecting a rental car—and then deciding what to do when we get there. If you are a veteran traveler, much of this process may be familiar, and you might wish to skim this section quickly.

As any reader will quickly see, I like to travel comfortably, yet I determinedly save money when I can. Although I no longer hitchhike or stay in youth hostels (a memory recalled, not always fondly, in My Love Affair with England*), I try to avoid the large, expensive hotels that cater to American tourists. So this is neither a bargain-basement nor a luxury guide, but a meandering path between the two—leading, I hope, to unusual places close to the heart of England.*

Do remember that prices and exchange rates fluctuate, hotels and B&Bs change management and even close, and your own discoveries may prove to be better than mine.

Months before we leave for England, I begin to travel. Night after night, I happily settle down with stacks of books, maps, and tattered clippings. Besides several current travel guides, I also gather together glossy picture books from the library or from my bookstore's cheap remainder tables. On a large pad of paper I list all the days we will be gone, one day per line, leaving space after each entry so I have room to make notes.

Now the work—and the fun—really begin. Curled up on the sofa, I sip my decaf, ponder my list of dates, open a map, and begin to dream. If we have sixteen days in England, where shall we go? What do I want to see and do? Where shall we stay and for how long? Thumbing through my books, I try to decide if we should return to Cornwall, which we love, or perhaps venture for the first time to the Northumbrian coast. Six days in north Norfolk, followed by one night on the road, then a week in the Border country? Or a week in Sussex, then a night in Dorset, and a second week on the north Devon coast? I jot various options on my list, tear the list up, and start another.

Would this perhaps be the time to try a week at the waterside cottage on the Thames sketched so charmingly in the National Trust handbook? Or should we find out if English Country Cottages still asks a reasonable rate in early April for the posh little hideaway in West Dorset once lived in by the Duchess of York? Should we divide our last two nights between luxurious Chedington Court and a farmhouse bed-and-breakfast in Dartmoor?

As I ponder all these tantalizing possibilities, and many more, I picture us having morning tea and scones on the roof terrace of Bar Lodge near Porthleven, Cornwall. I feel the crunch of the shingle beach as we trudge along under the formidable chalk cliffs of West Dorset. I see us rowing in a little skiff, like Mole and Ratty, along the meandering Thames. This is armchair traveling with an extra zest, for I know that I am actually going. Now it is just a question of when, where, and how—or, rather, it is *many* questions.

Looking up from my jumbled books and lists, I ask James, my husband, "Dear, do you think we should go back to Exmoor? Or return to Standen? Or would you rather try something new this time?" Unwilling to interfere, he usually smiles and shrugs. Within certain guidelines, he wants me to plan the trip. He doesn't want to bother to investigate all these alternatives. Once we're traveling, he'll gladly drive, take charge of luggage, and provide aid and comfort in tricky situations. He'll enthusiastically explore anywhere at any time. But right now I'm in charge.

Not everyone wants to be an amateur travel agent. Poring through books and maps takes commitment, time, and energy—and making crucial decisions can be scary. What if the hotel turns out to be dark and dreary, or plunked on a busy highway? (This has happened.) What if the cottage has a bathroom whose walls are covered with green mildew? (One cottage did.) Suppose the rented house has at least six different kinds of clashing carpet patterns? (We stopped counting at six.) If you travel with someone who is apt to say "Why didn't we stay at that nice Holiday Inn down the road?" or "Couldn't you *tell* from the brochure?" or "How much did you tell me we're paying for this dump?" then you may not want to be responsible.

Fortunately, James doesn't say any of those things. Not that he may not think them. As an architect, he is extraordinarily sensitive to the pleasantness of his surroundings—not poshness, but light, space, and charm. On the rare occasions when those are lacking, he has two main remedies. One is to march out, buy several bunches of fresh flowers, and strategically distribute them around our rooms. The other is to take a long, long walk, which usually gives him time to recover his equanimity and to remember that probably we'll be spending much of our time outdoors.

For us, the advantages of my being our travel agent far outweigh an occasional misjudgment. After all, even the most experienced professional planner can sometimes get it wrong too. And no one knows our tastes, dislikes, and whims as we do. By planning our own trips, we can explore byroads and odd places most commercial agents would never have heard of. I can construct an itinerary to take in gardens like East Lambrook and Clapton Court, the swannery at Abbotsbury, and the seaside promenade at the eighteenth-century seaside resort of Sidmouth. Or I can plot to visit a remote prehistoric stone circle, the New Age community of Findhorn on the northeast coast of Scotland, or the smallest church in England still open for occasional services. (On references to Scotland, see explanatory note in Section II, "Yes, I Know Scotland Is Not England.")

By serving as our travel agent, I also save us money. If we rent a "holiday flat" for a week, for example, we can stay in London in a small town house once owned by Sir John Betjeman, England's former poet laureate, with living room, kitchen, back terrace, bedroom, and full bath, within walking distance of the Barbican and St. Paul's, for under $85 a night in off season. (Although that may not sound cheap, try checking the cost of London hotels.) In a holiday flat, which comes completely furnished from sofa to saucepan, we can cook for ourselves. Just glancing at the prices on most London menus makes me lose my appetite—and besides, they don't always serve meals how or when we want them.

Outside London, expenses are even lower. In the country, a

three-bedroom cottage may rent for under $75 a night, and a farmhouse bed-and-breakfast for $35 or less per person. Last year in Scotland, we stayed one night in a genteel three-star Victorian hotel in the Highlands; using a half-price discount program we'd joined, we enjoyed an old-fashioned but comfy room with private bath and a full Scottish breakfast, from oatmeal and kippers to bacon and eggs, for a total of $71.

But perhaps my best reward for becoming involved—in fact, deeply immersed—in such detailed planning is being allowed to take a trip twice. The one I plan on paper is the ideal vacation, where everything works out just right. I have pleasure anticipating it for weeks. The second trip, when we actually go, is bumpier, messier, and full of surprises—but that, of course, is the one I will always remember.

"But how do you ever learn enough to make all these decisions? How do you actually go about it?" Sometimes when I try to encourage my friends to plan their own trips, they think the process is probably too difficult. But it isn't.

Where to Go?

It begins, I tell them, simply by deciding where they want to go. Whenever I travel, I always start out by reading as much as I can. I buy two or three general travel guides, the kind updated every year, familiar titles available in most bookstores. One isn't enough, because I want to compare notes on what each writer thinks about destinations, restaurants, and hotels. When I was devising an itinerary to the Highlands, for example, one guide merely mentioned the town of Drumnadrochit on Loch Ness as a "pleasant hamlet"; another cautioned: "If you are not put off by the traffic and the 'monster' tat [British for tackiness] which fills the place, Drumnadrochit is excellently situated." We did not stay in Drumnadrochit.

I also suggest to my friends that they buy one good touring map of England, just for planning general distances, and then several regional maps for the areas they may want to visit. The British Ordnance Survey series of maps has an exceptional range, not only geographically, but in type and size. (See Chapter Two, Draw Me a Map.) Other British map companies publish excellent leisure and touring maps too. Such maps will usually list tourist attractions, historic monuments, National Trust sites, famous gardens, and grand houses and castles open to the public. For anyone planning to drive for any distance, a road atlas is essential.

Where can you buy these maps? Some American bookstores, especially those in American cities, have travel sections that stock a variety of maps. Larger cities often have stores that specialize in maps; try MAPS in the Yellow Pages. An inquiring phone call to the geography department of a nearby college or university may turn up a local source, since a professional geographer will usually know where to buy good maps. BritRail's British Travel Shop, allied with the BritRail Travel International, may help too. (See "A Few Floating Facts" at the end of this chapter.) Finally, you can always write or call the Ordnance Survey in England and ask the name of your nearest dealer. (Again, see "A Few Floating Facts.")

In England, atlases and maps are often obtainable at Gatwick or Heathrow airport shops, and at almost any British bookshop. When I'm traveling in England, I often make a bookshop my first stop, so I can stock up on detailed maps I haven't been able to find at home, as well as maps for future trips.

All these guidebooks and maps add up in dollars and pounds, but those costs are very small compared to the total cost of the trip itself. Some sources of travel information are *not* expensive. Magazines and books from the library are free (but you can't mark them up, tear sections out, or take them with you on a long trip). Many major metropolitan newspapers have travel sections you can comb for relevant articles; the *New York Times* compiles its own index, which you can consult at your local library. The more information you can gather, the better your trip will be.

Every dollar spent on a good map—and a good British map may set you back $5, $10, or even more, a sum startling to Americans, who are used to cheap, if rudimentary, highway maps—will repay you many times over. You won't drive by the turnoff to the Bedgebury Pinetum, a park in Kent filled with rare conifers; you'll be prepared to stop at the Hawk Conservancy in Hampshire to watch a falcon in flight; you can seek out Aira Force, a beautiful waterfall in the Lake District; you can walk along the Camel Trail, following the lovely estuary of the Camel River in Cornwall. None of these places or walks will appear on a standard rental-car folding map of England, but they'll be easy to spot on your "Kent to Cornwall Holiday Map" or "A–Z Visitors Map of the Lake District" or "Ordnance Survey Landranger Map of Newquay, Bodmin, and Surrounding Area."

Let Your Fancy Be Your Guide!

As you consult maps and books in the planning process, I reassure my friends, you will soon get a general idea, a swift overview, of the different parts of England. Then, I tell them, rely on instinct. Go where you want to go, not where anyone else says you should. Let your fancy be your guide. If you've been curious about Cornwall ever since Daphne Du Maurier introduced you to its treacherous moorland and foaming seas, by all means spend time there, even if you don't see Stonehenge or Canterbury.

If your young heart once beat fast with Lorna Doone's, you may long to see Exmoor and the little church at Oare made famous in R. D. Blackmore's classic novel. Or perhaps you've heard so much about the Lake District that you're determined to retrace Wordsworth's footsteps, or Coleridge's, or Beatrix Potter's. You might be passionate about gardens; organize your trip around a half dozen or more, especially in Kent, Sussex, and the West Country. Or you could be a student of ley lines, crystals, reincarnation, and Arthurian legend, and you feel you absolutely must catch the New Age vibrations at Glastonbury. By all means go.

England offers such various pleasures that it can provide for all kinds of interests. I have known people who planned their trips around golf courses, fishing, museums featuring antique cars, World War II airplanes, Roman ruins, or fine-art printing presses. One reader wrote me wondering why I had never visited Liverpool. As an ardent Beatles fan, she had made that industrial city the focus of her trip, visiting Beatles landmarks and delighting in the friendliness, energy, and grit of the people she met. Another reader went only to Yorkshire, again and again, because she had so loved James Herriot's books. (Her devotion was rewarded; looking out the window of her rented cottage one morning, she actually saw the man himself walking his dog and rushed out to get his autograph.)

I have even planned a week's trip in England based on

nothing more substantial than the roll of a phrase. I had always liked the sound of "the north Norfolk coast," which created for me a sense of remoteness, unspoiled coastline, and little-known territory. (Of course I knew that like everywhere in England, it was not exactly the last frontier.) Indeed, as I began to read about the area, it did appear to be relatively unvisited by most American tourists. After finishing P. D. James's mystery, *Devices and Desires*, set on the north Norfolk coast, with a fierce gray sea beating in the background of almost every page, I knew I should go there. I did—and enjoyed myself immensely.

How Much Time to Allow?

Once I have decided where James and I will go, I plan how to spend the time we have set aside. We like to stay as long as possible in one place, preferably a week at a time, with perhaps a few traveling days at each end. This way we can get to know an area with a little depth. If we do not rent a cottage or flat for a week, we usually arrange more than one night at a destination. Since part of the first day is spent arriving, and most hotels or B&Bs expect their guests to leave in the morning of the second day, we need to spend two nights just to get one full day to explore. That calculation forms an excellent rule: two nights equals one day, three nights equals two days, and so on.

Since we travel by car in the countryside, I calculate our routes very carefully. I try to make each day a leisurely one, which means not more than a few hours in the car, if we are moving from point to point, or an hour at most if we are touring from a central base. I don't come to England to remain most of my day shut inside a moving vehicle.

Imagine me saying this in a very loud voice: ENGLAND MAY SEEM SMALL, BUT ITS DISTANCES ARE DECEPTIVE. It is impossible to overstress this warning. On a map, you may figure you can zoom sixty miles from point A to point B in an hour. But many roads are narrow and crowded, and some are *very* narrow, and others are *very* crowded. Instead of zooming down a lane, you may be crawling, while your companion in the passenger's seat (in our case, that's me) gulps as the hedgerow brushes the side of the car. Or you may find yourself stuck in what seems like rush-hour traffic at ten A.M. in the center of a town that you thought was too small to be a nuisance. England's old roads went right through the middle of all the action, and often they still do.

If you decide to take one of the M roads, England's version of freeways, you may make great time, provided you're not unnerved by cars racketing along at eighty or ninety (illegal) miles an hour. But weather and accidents can easily tie up those heavily used M roads, especially around large cities. We once took an hour to cover ten miles not far from the town of Stafford, south of Stoke-on-Trent. Irritable and worried about lost time, I told James to leave the M road at the next exit. Bad mistake. In minutes we were in the midst of an even worse tie-up with hundreds of other motorists trying to snake around the traffic knot. By the time we limped back to the freeway, even imperturbable James was beginning to mutter.

So I allot plenty of time, at least an hour for forty miles of open road, with an extra allowance then added for towns and for unforeseen stops—the medieval stone church whose graceful spire lures us into the market square, the signpost to a prehistoric fort a few miles off the road, the craft shop advertising hand weaving, James's sudden desire for a cup of coffee or mine for a cream tea.

Although we leave room for the unpredictable delights (and sometimes disasters) of each day, we always have a fixed itinerary. We know each night exactly where we'll stay. Years ago I used to wait until late afternoon to find a bed, but not anymore. We don't want to spend our all-too-precious time trying to find a hotel or B&B that is small, attractive, well located, quiet, and not too expensive. The ones that fill these criteria are usually booked well in advance. Now we're among the travelers who book them.

Where to Stay? What About Self-Catering?

How do we find those perfect (or almost perfect) places? Most of our vacation time in England is spent in furnished cottages or apartments, a mode of travel the British call *self-catering*. The easiest way to rent a furnished flat (British for *apartment*) or cottage is to contact an American agency that specializes in overseas vacation rentals. At least every year the Sunday *New York Times* runs one or more travel stories that list such agencies. *Consumer Reports Travel Letter* (see "A Few Floating Facts" at the end of this chapter) occasionally compiles a listing. A few upscale agencies advertise in magazines like *Travel and Leisure, Gourmet, The New Yorker, Travel Holiday*, and *Condé Nast Traveler*.

After calling one of these agencies and describing what you're looking for, you can often request and browse through a catalogue or list of possible properties. Some firms ask for a substantial up-front fee before you can register with them; others just charge a few dollars for the catalogue; some will copy certain pages from their listings and send them without charge. The firm's commission is included in the weekly rental fee. (Very few agencies will rent a property for less than a week, except during the depths of off season. But if you're going to England between November and early March, a three-day rental might be possible at some properties.)

After considering the properties on an agency's list, you can sometimes get a personal recommendation from someone who has visited the place. This can be enormously helpful. When we once rented in France, Carl Stewart, the owner of the small American agency with whom we dealt, told us, "No, no. I don't think you want that house you picked out of the catalogue. I can suggest another, much cheaper, you'll like better." From its photograph, we weren't impressed. But we took it, and it turned out to be a handsomely restored stone barn, converted and decorated by a professor and his wife for their own eventual retirement. It was a spacious, charming, and welcoming home. Carl had been there, and he knew.

After one or two phone calls, you may be able to settle on an appealing property and make a deposit. Then the agency handles all the other details. Shortly before you leave, they will send you a map, instructions about where and how to find a key, and any other information you may need. When your vacation is over, you are expected to leave your rental in decent condition, but your fee almost always covers a professional cleaning job. So you do not have to spend your last day vacuuming (or *Hoovering*, as the English might say).

Renting from an English Agency

Renting a cottage or flat from an American agency is the easiest way, but it is not the cheapest. Many American firms use the catalogue or list from an English affiliate and then add their own commission. You may wish to take some extra time and trouble, and to spend some modest sums on mail and phone calls, in order to rent directly from an English agency.

You then need to search out firms specializing in "self-catering holiday rentals." (Self-catering, remember, means a vacation rental that comes furnished and completely equipped. *Holiday* is a British term for vacation; a holiday rental is not just restricted to holidays like Christmas and Easter.) Many such agencies advertise in the London *Sunday Times* as well as in British and American magazines geared to travelers. You might try *British Heritage*, *Realm*, *In Britain*, *Country Life*, and other British magazines available at speciality newsstands in the States. The National Trust sends a quarterly magazine to its members; it has a large and appealing section of classified ads. (See "A Few Floating Facts.")

Call the agency in England (don't worry, they speak English!) and ask politely for their latest catalogue, sent immediately by air mail, or by a next-day express service if you're feeling extravagant. You can pay mailing costs by credit card. In fact, most agencies will let you conduct all your financial business with them with the right piece of plastic.

If you decide to stick with hotels and B&Bs on your next trip but hope to take another trip in a year or two and try self-catering then, you can also call those English agencies either from home or as soon as you've arrived in England and request catalogues to be sent to your last scheduled stop. This avoids both delays and transatlantic mailing costs.

Trust the Two Trusts!

I am devoted to two other sources of rental cottages and flats, the National Trust and the Landmark Trust, both of which have supplied us with marvelous places to stay. The National Trust, now the largest landowner in Britain, is best known for its preservation of historic places and areas of natural beauty. Almost every American who travels to England visits something owned by the National Trust, from Chartwell to Fountains Abbey to Sissinghurst Castle. But not many Americans know that the National Trust also rents out almost two hundred holiday cottages.

These rental properties range from a spacious stone lodge on the Cornwall cliffs to a riverside cottage on the Thames to a converted artist's studio in the Lake District. Since they all are situated on Trust property, sometimes even incorporated into one of the historic buildings, these accommodations are almost guaranteed to have unusual surroundings—and no unpleasant hidden surprises, like a fish and chips shop on the floor below, or a troop of plastic gnomes in the garden.

Each year the National Trust issues a new catalogue, with descriptions, color sketches, and photographs, and a price list. It is obtainable for a token cost at many National Trust shops in England and by mail. (See "A Few Floating Facts.") Just as with a commercial agency, you can use phone and credit card to make (or *book*) your reservation.

The Landmark Trust—not connected to the National

Trust—is a nonprofit organization that rescues buildings of architectural interest, restores them, and then rents them out. Many of their properties are fragments of former historic estates, or small buildings of great character but outmoded usefulness. So you have a chance to stay, for example, for a week or more in the Bath Tower, a late-thirteenth-century tower built into a medieval seawall in Caernarvon, Wales; the Pineapple, a fanciful summerhouse complete with prickly stone leaves, in Dunmore, Scotland; or Alton Station, a small railway station in Staffordshire.

Landmarks, as they are affectionately but respectfully known to their devotees, are furnished with great care, sometimes with antiques and Oriental carpets, always with discreetly tasteful furniture and with carefully chosen books. In 43 Cloth Fair in London, for example, the flat once owned by Sir John Betjeman, we could browse among books by and about Betjeman, as well as several about the neighborhood he lived in. Given their sense of historic atmosphere, it is not surprising that Landmarks do not provide television or telephone. But everything else is up-to-date.

The yearly Landmark catalogue is really a paperback book; big, thick, written with a dignified flair, professionally designed and illustrated, and relatively expensive. But it is worth every cent. (In 1995 it cost $19.50 if purchased from the Trust's American office, £8.50 if purchased in England.) Besides describing the history, significance, and style of each building and illustrating it with several black and white photographs, the catalogue locates it on a small inset map that shows other places of interest within a fifteen-mile radius.

Although the descriptions in most rental catalogues are usually quite short and pithy, the National Trust pamphlet manages to be both informative and evocative, and the Landmark Trust book, which devotes two pages to each property, is absolutely engrossing. I sometimes tuck both booklets into the magazine rack in my bathroom. What better way to while away a lazy, luxurious hour in the tub than by musing about the National Trust's Old Mill Cottage in the Severn Valley? "This fifteenth-century stone cottage lies in the heart of the wooded Herefordshire countryside. . . . Somewhat isolated, it is approached by means of a farm road to a hardstanding area for cars, and then by footbridge over a stream, with a further fifteen yards to the cottage door."

Or what about New Lodge in Trelissick, Cornwall? "With its rounded chimneys and latticed windows, this is a fascinating example of Victorian picturesque architecture." Or Diston's Cottage in the Cotswolds? "The home of the Diston family for three generations, this charming stone cottage with roses by the door has an old-fashioned stable door, from which you can watch the world go by, and a secluded garden."

Although the genteel Landmark Trust seldom gushes, its restrained prose is just as seductive. Who wouldn't yearn for the Swiss Cottage at Endsleigh, Devon? "The main room, opening onto a verandah, was always kept for the use of the Dukes for picnics and shooting lunches." Simplicity sounds irresistible in the Lettaford Chapel, a plain granite building in Devon: "Here two of you can cook, eat and sleep all in one big room, with an open fire. It has a little stream with flowery banks running close beside it." Far away from tourists, Purton Green, a medieval timber-framed hall-house, seems idyllic: "The house now stands surrounded by the life of the fields, with ordinary unchanging Suffolk countryside, marvelously unimproved, in all directions."

Not surprisingly, given their attractiveness and moderate cost (Landmarks from about $350 a week, in low season, to a top of about $3400 for a Devon manor house sleeping fifteen during Christmas week; National Trust properties generally from as little as $200 a week upward), the most popular holiday cottages in both catalogues are often booked months, even a year, in advance. But last-minute cancellations do occur, and you may be lucky, especially in spring and fall. All it takes is a phone call to find out.

May I Speak to Mrs. MacDonald, Please? Renting from Owners

The least expensive alternative in renting a self-catering cottage or flat is to contact an individual owner who does not list his or her property with any agency. This method does carry some risk, since an agency is supposed to inspect its listings regularly to assure their comfort, cleanliness, and safety, and you have no such guarantee with an individual rental. But you may be able to ask enough questions to allay any qualms.

To find individuals who are renting vacation homes, you can consult the classified section of the London *Sunday Times*, which carries a large number of travel ads. (Many metropolitan newsstands carry foreign newspapers, and some libraries order the *Times*.) College alumni magazines sometimes carry small ads, placed at little or no cost by subscribing alumni. The magazine from my own alma mater, Smith College, always has a selection of houses or apartments all over the world that other alumnae are willing to rent (and not just to Smith graduates).

Once you have decided upon the area in England where you want to stay, you can also contact the British Tourist Authority for available booklets or listings of self-catering accommodation. Or the B.T.A. might give you the address of the local tourist board, which will almost always have a list of hotels, B&Bs, and self-catering possibilities.

Even if you just write to "Tourist Information Centre" in the town where you'd like to stay, with no specific street address, your letter has a good chance of getting there. Be sure to enclose an international postal reply coupon, purchased from your post office. (It is easy to forget what it would cost a small office to airmail hundreds of overseas letters; someone there might be forced to forget to reply.)

Sometimes self-catering publications are sold as travel books in American bookstores. *Scotland Self-Catering*, a paperback guide we ordered from the Scottish National Tourist Board in Edinburgh, an organization that ranks hundreds of carefully inspected properties, is also on the shelf of one of my local independent bookstores. By checking ratings, locations, and other details in this guide, I was able to call several owners, ask questions (they asked some too), and confidently settle on a cottage and a flat, each for a week.

Both places, rented unseen, turned out to be absolutely splendid, with remarkable locations and views, impeccable cleanliness, and all the *mod cons* (British for modern conveniences, such as microwave, dishwasher, even a Cuisinart). These properties had earned the tourist board's highest ratings, whose stars and crowns are doled out very sparingly. Yet, because we were renting directly from the owners, the cost was probably half what we'd have had to pay an agency.

Most individual owners do not, of course, take credit cards

for deposits. We solved the problem of how to avoid the cost of changing currencies twice for deposit and final payment by sending a deposit check in dollars to the owners, asking them to hold it until our arrival, and then paying them in full in British currency. (This way, if a renter defaulted, the owner could still cash the check.)

Deciphering the Catalogues

Most tourist board listings of self-catering properties do not include photographs, although a few owners pay extra to have their properties pictured. (Sometimes an individual owner will consent to send you photographs if you promise to return them.) But whether it is from a commercial agency, the National or Landmark Trust, or a tourist board, a catalogue of rental properties is to me, like the old Sears Roebuck catalogue, a dream book. Even without illustrations, a catalogue can create castles in the sky from cottages on the ground.

When a catalogue arrives, I can never resist dropping everything in order to page through it. As I study the pictures and/or description of each house or flat, I try to envision us inside. Then I struggle to decipher the cryptic language and coded symbols that describe each property: number and kind of rooms, type of bathroom (shower or tub), size and equipment of kitchen, type of heating (and who pays for it), the day of the week rentals begin (usually Friday or Saturday), and other essential facts. (Each catalogue provides a key for cracking this code.)

I have learned to inquire about several facts *not* always listed too. Is the cottage on a main road? Or how far away from a main road? We do not want *lorries* (trucks) rumbling under our bedroom window. If the cottage is on the grounds of an owner's larger house, how far away is the other house? (We cherish our privacy.) Are linens (sheets and towels) included? Or can they be rented for a modest fee? (We have occasionally schlepped a bag of sheets and towels along with us, but it is a nuisance.)

A single picture can tell a great deal. From an exterior shot we can often judge how light or dark the house will be, depending on the size and number of its windows. Are the bedrooms all upstairs? If the house has a sharply gabled second story, then those bedrooms may be lit only by small windows tucked under the eaves.

Interior photographs are also revealing. If the lumpy-looking sofa and matching armchair are covered in a bilious green tweed, with a few toss pillows in murky brown florals, next to a tilting floor lamp with a rakishly fringed maroon shade, we can predict what the rest of the interior will be like. Some owners evidently buy furniture for their rental houses as if they were expecting drunken college students on a destructive binge. Other owners mean well but have terrible taste. A few, happily, furnish their properties as if they actually want to attract visitors. We look for those.

If you like a little light and space in your bathroom, study the notations in the listing carefully. Americans use the word bathroom to refer to a room with toilet; the English are very specific about whether a room has a WC (water closet, or toilet), a shower, a bathtub, or all of the above. A room with *H & C* will merely have a sink with hot and cold running water. A shower room may indeed have only a shower in it, nothing else. Such a cubicle is likely to be a converted closet, not exactly a pleasant place to lounge about. A room with a bathtub is bound to be larger.

Finally, ponder the phrase *en suite*. To the English, this indicates that some kind of space with a toilet is attached to the bedroom, so you do not need to go out into the hall to a separate room. This is handy, of course, when you get up in the middle of the night. But en suite can also imply that in order to provide guests with this certifiable private facility, an owner has jerry-rigged a flimsy closetlike space, with tissue-paper walls, from a corner of the bedroom. We are often happier to traipse down the hall to a room that is *not* en suite.

I have also learned to read certain entries as potential red flags. A cottage that is *purpose-built* means something new, probably without character, rather like a small tract house. *Chalet*, though it sounds romantically Swiss, usually refers to a generic A-frame or precut cabin, also quite new, often plopped down in multiples, like a tourist camp, on a bare piece of property without any shading trees or garden. *Garden*, by the way, does not always mean a large plot of flowers and shrubs; the English use garden the way we do *yard*. A house that "sits in its own small garden" may merely indicate that it has some green around it.

Americans should not expect forced-air heat or radiators controlled by one thermostat, the kind of central heating we know best. "Heating by electric fires" probably uses small portable electric heaters, not very effective in keeping large spaces warm. *N.S.* or night storage heaters are large metal radiator-type enclosures with interior units that store up heat at night and release it slowly during the day. (Under this arrangement, one's bedroom can be quite chilly at night, and on warm summer days, rather stuffy.) Costs of fuel and electricity are sometimes extra in self-catering rentals. It pays to ask, for the cost of keeping warm can be quite chilling.

An *Aga*, often mentioned as a point of pride, is somewhat like an old-fashioned kitchen range, with the kind of flat iron top and removable lid griddles I remember on my grand-mother's wood stove. Since an Aga is always on, heating not only its stovetop but also the room around it, it can be quite cozy on a cold morning in the kitchen. In England, except in the case of a record-breaking heat wave, you will never need an air conditioner outside the city. (And if you need one, you won't get one anyway.)

Preparing for Cook's Night In

Almost every self-catering rental has a fully equipped kitchen with a stove (often quite small), a refrigerator (usually a third the size of an American one with a tiny ice cube compartment instead of a freezer), an electric teakettle, various pots and pans, tools, and utensils. Coffeemakers are relatively rare. Either bring your own (perhaps a coffee cone with filters), settle for instant, or drink tea.

Although you do not really need to pack most supplies, I travel with what I call my kitchen bag—a small satchel. James and I both like to cook (and eat), and I want to make my life in the kitchen as easy as possible. Sometimes I find leftover provisions from previous tenants, but many housekeepers clean so thoroughly that even salt and pepper disappear. In terms of edibles, assume nothing.

In my kitchen bag I tuck little plastic bags filled with favorite herbs, a cup or so of flour for breading fish, a bit of sugar for James's cereal and coffee, portable salt and pepper shakers, a jar of garlic salt, my favorite vegetable peeler, a roll of tinfoil and another of plastic wrap, a dish sponge and a piece of steel wool, a small plastic bottle of dish detergent, bars of soap (not always supplied in rental houses), and several folded-up plastic trash bags.

Cooking for ourselves, we often have leftovers. So I also take a stash of pint- and quart-size plastic bags (good for storing dampish items in a suitcase too) and a few plastic storage containers, all of which weigh almost nothing. These are handy when we pack a picnic lunch. Juice in England usually comes in square cardboard boxes which spill easily when opened, so I take a quart-size screwtop plastic jar.

Our final and most essential add-on is a medium-size, freshly sharpened kitchen knife. No vacation rental ever supplies a good, sharp one. But be sure to pack this in a suitcase that you plan to check. To my embarrassment and James's amusement, I was once abruptly stopped by the security guard at Gatwick. After watching my carry-on pass through the X-ray machine, the guard looked at me quizzically, unzipped my bag, and carefully removed a lethal-looking knife with an eight-inch blade. "Is this yours?" he inquired in an unsurprised tone, as if most middle-aged, fairly well-dressed ladies usually carried large knives with them when they boarded planes.

What About Hotels?

If you do not want to spend a week in one spot, or you shudder at the idea of having to cook at all on your vacation, or you long for the friendly ambience of a bed-and-breakfast, then you open a different field of investigation. Even when we are self-catering, James and I do stay in two or more hotels or B&Bs on each trip. Seldom can we drive straight from the airport to a self-catering property deep in the countryside, at least not without a certain level of stress from an overnight on the plane.

Choosing a hotel or B&B has its own pleasures. Just as I love to browse through catalogues of rental properties, I also enjoy reading about hotels and B&Bs. We may stay in only one or two places, but I try out a dozen or more in my mind.

If we decide to stay in a hotel, I usually begin by looking in the booklet published by a discount program to which we belong. Several such programs exist; they are regularly described and rated in *Consumer Reports Travel Letter*. (See "A Few Floating Facts.") Ours costs $53 a year, and it provides us with an annual list of hotels in Europe that have agreed to offer deep discounts, usually fifty percent off the regular, or *rack*, rate to its members. (We also belong to another program that lists hotels in America, with a few from Europe thrown in. Sometimes that program carries names the other one doesn't.)

Using the program is simple. I call or fax the hotel we've selected, ask if our program's rate is available on a particular date, and, if so, make a reservation. We travel enough so the $53 annual fee is a bargain, but even if we used the program just once, it would be quite satisfying to an Iowa-born scrounger (me) to pay only $75 for a room that costs regular tourists $150.

Certain restrictions can apply. If a hotel is almost full, or expects to be, it obviously doesn't need to offer a discount, and it won't. Sometimes the discounted rooms may be less desirable than nondiscounted rooms. Occasionally a hotel will require a two-night stay, or limit the discount to specified days of the week. But we have usually been pleased with our half-price program, and several of the hotels we've used have been deluxe, even stunning, places to stay.

The discount booklet says very little about a hotel except its name, size, location, and relative cost, usually indicated by category as low, moderate, or high. (To get the precise room rate, I have to call, fax, or write.) So the process I follow to select a hotel at discount is the same one I use for any other hotel: diving into guidebooks. I consult several, cross-checking what each has to say about the same hotel. A flood of books appears every year on England's small hotels, country hotels, So-and-So's Recommended Hotels. (Remember, you don't need to buy all these guides; use your library, and browse in friendly bookstores.)

What do I look for? In England, we usually prefer an older hotel, not a brand-new one. If a description doesn't tell you whether a hotel is old or new, its picture will. An older hotel probably has more character, and its rooms may be larger, with taller ceilings and generous windows that open for fresh air. In general, we also like smaller hotels, which have a more personal feeling, and usually more distinctiveness. A hotel with ten rooms is probably a converted house or mansion; a hotel with three hundred rooms is like an office building.

In a city I want a hotel close to the center, within easy walking distance of restaurants, museums, and theaters. I always ask for a room as high up as possible, in the back, to avoid street noise. In the country I search out hotels with large yards, set if possible in several acres of grounds, or at least located well away from the highway.

Avoid, if you can, any hotel whose address includes *High Street*. This is Main Street, a commercial route and probably a highway through town as well, and traffic will boom along it day and night. Even in a small town, the High, as it is known, may be surprisingly busy. Once in Arundel, a pleasant town near the south coast, we booked a nice-sounding hotel on the High for two nights. Our first night, a zillion-watt streetlight shone through our gauzy curtain right onto my pillow. Through the thin single-paned window, I could hear motorcycles racing along the High, lorries thundering by, and cars sputtering through faulty mufflers. We did not stay a second night, and arranging a change was a time-consuming bother.

Study hotel brochures carefully. Does the road run right in front of the door? Does the furniture look tacky? Is any bedroom pictured? (If the brochure proudly displays photos of the foyer, dining room, and sitting room but not a single bedroom, you can bet the hotel probably doesn't have a bedroom it wants to show off.) If a bedroom *is* pictured, does it seem to be an average double, like the one you'd get, or is it a one-of-a-kind honeymoon suite?

Almost all hotels these days quote rates that include VAT (Value Added Tax), and service charge, but read the fine print just to make sure. A few hotels still offer an English breakfast as part of the deal, which means a full range of juice, eggs, bacon, cereal, and other goodies. *Continental* breakfast will probably be juice, some sort of roll, and coffee. If breakfast is extra, it may be quite expensive; be prepared to look elsewhere. We often pack a few six-ounce cans of juice for just such occasions, and we make up the rest of our meal from nearby shops, probably baked rolls or croissants fresh from a bakery, followed by tea and coffee at any convenient restaurant or tea shop.

The Pleasures of B&Bs

Most Americans who travel in England are struck by the astonishing number of signs announcing BED AND BREAKFAST or the common shorthand, B&B. A B&B may be run either by an owner who lets out one or more rooms in his or her private home or by an innkeeper who has converted a large house into a small hotel. As its name indicates, a B&B includes breakfast in its cost; it may or may not provide a private toilet and/or bath. Attractive choices for budget-conscious travelers, B&Bs often offer an informal, homey atmosphere; rooms with individualized charm and furnishings; quiet, out-of-the-way settings; and delicious breakfasts.

Of course a B&B can be dreary, its rooms quite small, and the surroundings depressingly suburban. So I choose a B&B just as carefully as a hotel, by consulting several guidebooks, such as *The Best Bed and Breakfast in the World* (a somewhat misleading title, since all listings are in fact in Britain) or *AA Inspected Bed and Breakfast in Britain* (with awards for "best newcomers") or *Consumer Reports' The Bed and Breakfast Guide to Great Britain* or *Where to Stay: Farmhouses, Bed & Breakfast Inns and Hostels*, published by the English Tourist Board, with ratings of inspected properties.

When selecting a B&B, I make note of the number of *public* bathrooms compared to bedrooms. The public bath (not, of course, open to the general public!) is the one shared by rooms that do not have a bathroom en suite (attached to the room), and I am not eager to stand too long in line. I also avoid bungalows, whose rooms are often quite modest in size, and whose architecture is probably cookie-cutter contemporary. Instead, I look for listings like "very quiet sixteenth-century stone farmhouse with interior oak beams," or "magnificently converted eighteenth-century Kentish barn," or "house set in seven acres of ornamental gardens"—all phrases I've plucked from the B&B guidebooks mentioned above.

We usually try to avoid arranging in advance for the evening meal, which some proprietors offer and a few require. The cost is usually fairly high, and the food often mediocre— a pale slab of meat, soggy potatoes, overcooked vegetables, and a hunk of pie made with canned apples. Good cooks do run B&Bs, but they are rare. Almost anywhere in England we can find a pub or restaurant that will give us a choice of menu, at an hour of our choosing, not the set hour of the residential meal.

A *farmhouse* B&B is a misleading term to many Americans, for it conjures up visions, at least for me, of a stark white house, square and plain, set amid rolling fields. But in England, a farmhouse might be a handsome and spacious home of character. It might not even be on what we might think of as a working farm. Great Wapses Farm, where we once stayed, near Henfield in West Sussex, was a sort of hobby farm, with horses and ducks, a delightful pond and garden, and a house that was an attractive mixture of Tudor and Georgian architecture.

Neither farmhouse nor B&B accommodation is necessarily cheap, although it usually is less than a hotel. Prices have risen in recent years, and we now expect to pay about $60, sometimes more, for our room and breakfast, although we have been pleasantly surprised by less.

Cook's Night Out: Survival Tips for Eating in England

Even if you stay in a self-catering cottage or flat, you will still want to eat some meals outside your own kitchen. Any well-stocked bookshop in England can sell you a guide to restaurants (*The Good Food Guide* is a standard) and the general, all-purpose guidebooks often suggest some too. But you may not be able to plan your day, or trip, around culinary recommendations, and impromptu meals can sometimes turn out to be both dreary and expensive.

When in doubt, choose an omelette. The English excel in cheeses of all kinds, and their eggs seem to be especially tasty too. Few cooks can really spoil an omelette, and although it is not exactly a low-calorie, low-cholesterol dish, it can be meltingly delicious, with bits of ham, onion, tomato, or other ingredients folded into the creamy egg and cheese. An omelette almost always comes with a bit of salad on the side, usually the tender green lettuce we call Boston and they call English, and perhaps a bit of tomato and *cress*, tiny sprouts with a mild onion flavor, as well.

The term *salad* can be misleading in England. Ham salad or turkey salad does *not* mean a chopped-up mixture of ham with lots of mayonnaise, the kind of dish served at old-fashioned ladies' luncheons in America. In England, salad as a main dish usually refers to a plate with a slice of ham (or turkey, beef, etc.), and several relishes plunked down next to it—perhaps a pear chutney, or canned corn and tomato chunks, or an indescribable mixture of something with pickles. (*Gammon* salad is not a plate of some kind of fish, as I once mistakenly thought, but smoked ham with relishes on the side.)

Although a few American-style fast food restaurants are springing up along British highways, we much prefer to take our chances with a pub lunch. As most American visitors to England know, the English pub is a social institution, subject these days to much change and criticism, but still going strong. Almost all pubs offer food from a short menu either posted or handed out at the bar. You order at the bar, then perch at little tables, next to patrons who are perhaps just downing a pint or two, and wait till someone brings your food. Neither service nor food is fancy, but your meal will be reasonably quick, sometimes freshly cooked (and sometimes microwaved), and relatively inexpensive.

The cheapest choice at a pub is usually soup and a roll, served as an entree, which at its best can mean a hearty, home-made bowl of chicken and vegetable or split pea with ham, together with a large, fresh brown roll and a slab of creamy butter. Of course, it can also mean a bowl of lukewarm tomato juice and a stale roll that is turning to concrete before your eyes. Pub lunches carry no guarantees; I always order a glass of sweet cider, just in case. (Be warned, however: English cider is not the harmless stuff sold in American supermarkets or commercial orchards. It is both delectable and definitely alcoholic.)

Another way to get a good lunch on the road is to stop at a supermarket or the shops on High Street. Look for signs advertising FRESH-CUT SANDWICHES, which usually include ham, cheese, egg salad, tuna fish, and possibly smoked salmon. These sandwiches are so well wrapped that they do taste as if someone had just slathered them together in the kitchen; the bread is fresh and the filling moist.

Most grocers, even the smallest village shops, also carry individual cartons of such deli items as cole slaw, potato salad, yogurt, and pudding, not to mention fresh fruit, local cheese, and an assortment of crackers. Butchers often stock individual quiches, meat pies, and sausage rolls, and bakers might provide many of the same items, as well as bread, rolls, cookies, and tarts.

With such resources, you'll find do-it-yourself picnics very easy and inexpensive. You might want to add to your front-seat supply bag a few plastic spoons, napkins or paper towels, and a vegetable peeler (for instant carrot sticks). Afterward you can watch for a roadside van selling tea and coffee.

How Do We Get There? Rental Cars

Once we've found the best places to stay and eat, how do we get to them? Outside of London, we drive. Or, rather, James drives. I'm timid enough on American highways; I'd hyperventilate the minute I slid into a left-hand driver's seat. So I sit next to him with a bag of maps and guidebooks on the floor by my feet and with at least one map spread out on my lap. "Think left!" I cry as we make a sudden turn. "In a few minutes watch for the turnoff to the M25!" "We ought to be coming soon to the A303 toward Andover, so be prepared!" "I'm not sure which way yet. Go around again!"

"Go around again" means we have just entered a roundabout, an ingenious but often confusing British device for arranging an intersection. Basically, it is a traffic circle that two or more roads enter from different directions. As you circle in multiple unmarked lanes, you look for a sign that points to the road where you want to peel off.

The one tip James gives first-time drivers in England is to

remember to *give way to the right* when entering a round-about. As official map-reader and adviser, I add, "And remember that once you're in a roundabout, you can just keep going around until you know where to turn."

Knowing where to turn isn't always easy. British road signs can often be infuriating, sometimes placed too late to see until you've passed the necessary exit, or not placed anywhere at all. They can assume a detailed knowledge of geography most visitors don't have. For instance, I might spot a sign at the side of the road that says BEAMINSTER 12, and then, when we enter the next roundabout a few miles later, I don't find any directions to Beaminster at all. Instead, I see signs for Axminster or Exeter or Dorchester.

While I frantically search the map to see whether Beaminster and Axminster are on the same highway, I wail at James, "No, no! Don't turn off! Just keep going around!" Sometimes he placidly circles two or three times, seemingly unfazed by the fluid lines of traffic weaving around us as I decipher our route.

But beyond a few such tense moments, we both feel that touring by car is the way we prefer to explore England. We can drive to out-of-the-way places, meander down country roads, and stop when and where we wish. Before I met James, who, as he proudly says, is the son of a rural mailman, and who therefore will drive almost anywhere under any conditions, I traveled through England by train and by foot. Having the freedom to go almost anywhere by car has been an undreamed-of luxury.

Of course I still encourage friends who are too terrified of driving in England to travel by whatever means they can manage. I have heard of people who tour exclusively by train, bus (not just tour buses or *coaches*, but regularly scheduled country and intercity buses), as well as by limo, canal boat, bicycle, and even mail delivery vans. But I prefer the independence and freedom of our car.

Just as I choose our places to stay, I arrange our car rentals very carefully. Since touring by car is not cheap—gas, or *petrol* in Britain is very expensive to Americans—I try to find the best deal possible. I quickly learned that all car rental agencies are not alike. In fact, almost every one will quote a different rate for exactly the same kind of car and the same length of time.

Although some travelers assume that they have the choice of only three or four internationally based car rental firms, there is in fact quite a large and competitive group. *Consumer Reports Travel Letter* and sometimes other travel magazines or newspaper travel sections periodically list agencies that rent cars in Europe, giving comparative pricing policies and phone numbers. Many large agencies have names most tourists have never heard of. But they are worth getting to know, because they subcontract excess cars from some of the better-known firms and then rent them at substantially less. These bargain agencies usually have what are called *off airport* locations (though not always), with a van that transports clients from the airport to a nearby office a few miles away.

The car rental firms solid enough to merit our confidence all have toll-free 800 numbers. On our last trip to England, I called *twelve* different firms for quotations on a ten-day rental of a midsize four-door car, nonautomatic, to be picked up and returned at Gatwick. No price fixing here: Every single one of the twelve price quotations was different, varying from a few dollars to $212. (Spending an hour on the phone saved us that $212, and did I feel smug.)

On our first trip to England we ordered a car with automatic transmission, which is much more expensive—shockingly expensive—than a manual, because James had been driving an automatic at home for years. He was concerned that he'd have trouble mastering the left-hand driving routine at the same time he polished up his old skills at shifting gears. But after that first trip he decided the price differential wasn't worth it. He has always driven a manual shift since and has felt quite comfortable with it.

We always request a slightly larger car than the lowest or subcompact class—usually what is called a midsize, but which Americans might know as a compact—for comfort and for luggage space. We also request a car with four doors so we can retrieve suitcases, lunch sacks, and coats from the backseat with relative ease. (Someone else might rather save a few dollars and scrunch up a bit.) Midsize cars in England often come equipped with not only radio but tape deck, and a final driving tip is to take a few favorite, soothing tapes to use during traffic tie-ups or long hauls on hilly roads where the BBC fades away.

On-the-Spot Planning

Although I have always read enough in guidebooks and other travel literature so I know something of what I want to see—a famous garden, a country house, a scenic vista (which the British refer to as "a beauty spot")—I leave plenty of room for spur-of-the-moment stops. Since I carry a large-scale tourist map in the car, it locates all sorts of intriguing local attractions. I can watch for an operating watermill, a waterfowl preserve, a fragment of a medieval tower, a group of prehistoric burial chambers, a historic battlefield, or a butterfly museum and silk farm. (These have all been stops we're glad we didn't miss.)

I carry a copy of the National Trust annual handbook in my front-seat satchel. The Trust owns properties everywhere, from Virginia Woolf's former home at Rodmell, East Sussex, to St. Michael's Mount, a spectacular castle on a rock in Cornwall. If our annual membership has expired, I renew it at the first National Trust site we visit. (Americans actually join an affiliate called Royal Oak, with the same privileges but a different name.)

Although the annual fee may seem large (about $40 in 1995 for a single membership), we have found that within a two-week visit, even less, we would easily spend that much on separate admissions. Stourhead Garden, for example, would have cost us £4.20 each in 1995; Sissinghurst, £5; Standen House, £4; Wakehurst Place Gardens, £4; Cotehele, £5. With our entrance card in hand, we are more likely to stop at lesser-known places too, or revisit our favorites, since we have the pleasant (if slightly misleading) sensation that we are getting in free. We also have the assurance that we are supporting an excellent cause, the preservation of much that we come to England to enjoy.

Since I love English gardens, I also travel with the *Good Gardens Guide*, which lists, rates (up to two stars), and describes more than a thousand gardens worth visiting, with clear and complete directions about how to find each one. As we drive along, I make sure we can at least consider stopping at every possible garden along the way.

Another crucial guidebook for garden lovers is the yearly

edition of *Gardens of England & Wales*, published by the National Gardens Scheme. This inexpensive paperback opens the
door to more than three thousand private gardens whose
owners participate in the National Gardens Scheme by welcoming the public for one or more days a year, with the admission fees going to a specified charity.

The N.G.S. guidebook handily lists these openings both by
county and by month, so, if you happen to be driving through
Kent in August, you can look up KENT, quickly check the
dates you'll be in that county, see what gardens will be open
then, and refer to the listings to see just where each one is.
Most openings occur, understandably, on weekends in the
spring, summer, and early fall.

The very short descriptions give little idea of the character
of the garden, so each one comes as an almost complete surprise. One Saturday morning in April, I saw in the N.G.S.
guide that a nearby garden called Glassenbury Park was open
that day. All the guide said was: "50 acres rolling parkland.
Newly planted daffodils and tulips. Specimen trees, rhododendrons, azaleas. Wide variety newly planted trees. Ponds
and lakes." This was certainly a tight-lipped entry. But I liked
the sound of fifty acres of rolling parkland, and Glassenbury
Park was almost directly on our way home from Sissinghurst.
So we added it to our day's schedule.

When we came to the end of the long private drive to
Glassenbury, we could look down upon the deep secluded
hollow of the park, whose acres of manicured green lawn surrounded an imposing mansion. Its warm but faded red brick,
added wings, and many chimneys suggested a heritage several
centuries old. Although the house itself was not open to view,
we were able to walk all around it and admire the black swans

in its moat. Just having the opportunity to see the house in its lovely setting was more than worth our short detour (plus a mere £2 admission for charity).

The owner, whom we unexpectedly met as we strolled through the park, told us he had lost more than eight hundred trees in the storm of 1987; several thousand had now been replanted. Yet the grounds still seemed wooded to us, probably because we could see no other buildings, just the stately house among grass and trees. Flowering rhododendrons on the side of the hill cast a bright pink glow over the rain-washed green lawns. This was more than just "rolling parkland." As for "newly planted daffodils," the gardeners at Glassenbury had recently put in more than fifty thousand, a display that shone like small golden stars. Without our N.G.S. guide, we would have missed all of it.

Keeping an Eagle Eye Out

As chief navigator and map-reader, it is also my responsibility to watch for unexpected opportunities. When my mother took my sister and me as children on family car trips, she called this "keeping an eagle eye out." In England I look not only for gardens but for *jumble* (rummage) sales, *car boot* sales (rummage in a car trunk), village *fetes* (fairs, charity bazaars, and festivals) and *coffee mornings* (local fund-raising events with coffee, baked goods, and assorted treats).

If James and I are lucky enough to spy a handmade sign on a tree or fence post announcing an open garden nearby, we can rarely resist following its beckoning arrows. One sunny Sunday in Cornwall, as we were heading toward the town of

Truro, I noticed a placard by the side of the road: CARCLEW GARDENS OPEN. Although I quickly consulted my various guidebooks, I could find no mention of any such garden. This was an invitation I felt we could not miss.

Turning off the road, we drove slowly down a narrow lane for several miles, long enough so that I became uneasy, wondering if Carclew Gardens really existed. Then the lane narrowed farther into a private drive, barely wide enough for a single car, shadowed by overarching trees. When we emerged into sunshine again, we were near a very old brick stable. A genial man in tweeds waved us toward a parking area just outside the stable. We had arrived.

Carclew Gardens, which had been opened for the day under the auspices of yet another organization, the Cornish Gardens Trust, might have fittingly surrounded the castle of Sleeping Beauty. Dwarfing the house and threatening to become entirely impenetrable, the garden seemed to have grown far beyond its original design. Part was now almost a forest of huge, tangled rhododendrons tumbling down a hillside in riotous color.

Under dark, glossy leaves, we followed a path that led us to a large ornamental pond, entirely cloaked by trees and the flowering rhododendrons. Imposing and formal, with two spouting fountains in the shape of sea gods, the pool also seemed overgrown, with an air of benign neglect. Green algae and lily pads covered most of the murky water. But the pool still had an impressive air, as if expecting the startled gasps of every new visitor who pushed aside a branch and suddenly stepped out into the light-filled enclosure.

Another path led us to an old, intricately carved stone bench. Although it may have once been a sought-after retreat, it was now almost swallowed up by the arms of giant rhododendrons. The moss-covered seat was covered with dead leaves, and anyone who scooped a place to sit down would find herself staring directly into thick, dark bushes.

The atmosphere of Carclew followed us beyond its borders. Not far from the garden, on a barred side road from whose gate we could only stand and peer, stood a monumental ruin, two stories of vine-covered columns and pediment. This classical façade was the remnant of the original house that had burned down several decades ago. (See another mention of Carclew in Chapter Nine, Hidden Corners in Du Maurier Country.)

Treasures at the Tourist Information Centre

If we had not seen the sign to Carclew and followed it, we would have missed one of the most evocative gardens of that entire trip. But I do not simply depend on luck. Whenever we arrive in a town where we'll stay for more than a day, I search out the local Tourist Information Centre. There I gather all the leaflets, booklets, and maps that seem even remotely useful. Next I find a bookshop and search its shelves for other local publications helpful to tourists. That night after supper, I sit down with my maps and materials, much as I did when I first began to plan our trip, and survey all our possibilities.

In bookshops I have found titles like *Woodland Walks in South-West England*, part of a series covering all the woodlands of England, Scotland, and Wales. *Walks from Your Car* and *Walks for Motorists* are also guidebooks in series that delineate easy circular walking tours in different parts of England. The Countryside Commission's National Trail Guides describe and map sections of long-distance footpaths.

The Ordnance Survey publishes local guides as well. *Southwest Coast Path: Padstow to Falmouth* faithfully escorted us along a section of coastline where we were staying for a week. (As a bonus, such a guidebook, tucked into a homeward-bound suitcase, will later bring back memories of windswept clifftops, sheltered lagoons, sand dunes, and long sea vistas.)

Some of the best books and pamphlets are very local indeed. *The Vegetarian Guide to the Scottish Highlands and Islands*, for example, was an invaluable manual of restaurants and cafés serving more than fish and chips, smoked salmon salad, or Scotch beef. *Welsh Walks and Legends: South Wales* entertained us with eighteen tales that included a miraculous cow, a heroic cuckoo, and a thwarted devil, while outlining walks where each legend took place. *Walks Around Crewkerne*, published by a local walkers' group, revealed footpaths and circular routes near that small Dorset town.

At Tourist Information Centres I often glean valuable small nuggets. At Inverness, for example, rifling through a rack of handouts, I unearthed one brochure that led us to a guided tour of Culloden Moor by costumed amateur actors, on one of only three dates the White Cockade Society would perform. (See Chapter Seventeen, Two Scottish War Memorials.)

Another leaflet from my Inverness cache listed that month's programs at the Eden Court Theatre, the city's main stage and concert hall. So the next Thursday night, we joined a crowd of dressed-up Scots for "A Gala Evening of Music to Commemorate the 50th Anniversary of the Battle of the Atlantic," a benefit in aid of King George's Fund for Sailors. A resplendent full-dress band of thirty-five Royal Marines, highly polished in sound as well, began with a rousing Sousa march, threw in sea songs and jazzed-up Bach, and almost blew the top off the hall with a medley of big-band oldies. All the way home we competed for the loudest chorus of: "He's the Boogie-Woogie Bugle Boy of Company B"!

Although I had planned during our stay near Inverness to take a boat trip on Loch Ness, a popular excursion widely touted in guidebooks, the morning we'd set aside for this three-hour voyage turned out to be cold and rainy. I wasn't at all sure I wanted to peer out fogged-up windows merely in the hope of seeing the elusive Nessie. So I pulled another handout from the Information Centre pile and suggested to James we take a look at *Amazon*, the museum ship, instead.

Amazon, originally built in 1885, is an elegant private yacht built for sail and steam, and now under total restoration by its owner, Stephen Lowe, whose father, the much-loved comic actor Arthur Lowe, acquired it twenty-five years ago. Between April and October, Stephen Lowe opens it for inspection at its mooring on a canal just outside Inverness.

Winding through the outskirts of Inverness, finding the right stretch of canal—a lonely gray ribbon of water with only a shuttered cottage at the nearby lock—and edging onto its grassy bank to park, we knew we had left the Inverness tourist trail far behind us. As the rain beat steadily down on our umbrellas, we made a dash from our car to the deck of the *Amazon*—and, as happens on so many of our slightly offbeat excursions, we found ourselves the only tourists there.

Mr. Lowe himself, hard at work in his coveralls, showed us around the vintage yacht. A ship with beautiful lines and a graceful curving sweep, it was made of pitched pine below the water, teak above. Below the decks, pitch-pine panels with teak surrounds gave the cabin a dark opulence. Brass and copper fittings were polished to perfection, the galley was a marvel of tidiness and ingenious arrangements, and even the full-size Victorian bathtub gleamed.

Being occasionally privileged to share someone's passion, however briefly, is one of the rewards of independent travel. Mr. Lowe, who had served in the merchant navy, clearly loved ships and the sea, and the *Amazon* was his personal pride. He brought out the line drawings of the ship, *lifted* (to a nonseaman, copied or drawn to accurate scale) by a naval architect who was a friend of his. He displayed photographs from *Amazon*'s heyday, yellowed newspaper clippings, and bits of miscellany that illustrated the yacht's history.

We felt as if Mr. Lowe had ushered us into his private home, and in a way, he had. In a tiny bunk room, a canvas cot hung from four metal rings, providing space for the Lowes' baby during the periods they lived full-time on the yacht.

Mr. Lowe's desire to restore the *Amazon* to its original state knew no bounds. Opening the door to the head, or WC, he showed us a flush toilet, but he hoped to replace it, he said, with the original bucket contrivance. "People today care more about convenience than about esthetics," he said with regret. That, James and I agreed later, was commitment.

On the way back to our cottage that noon, we drove along the shore of Loch Ness until we found a spot where we could pull over, admire the impressively gloomy lake and its wooded hills, and eat a picnic lunch in our car. As we stared out over the black, wind-rippled water, we saw the tourist boat puffing its slow way down the middle of the lake. It looked cold, wave-tossed, and almost deserted. No one was on deck. If I had not known about the *Amazon*, we might have been among those huddled inside.

Suppose you don't want to tour a vintage yacht? You can easily find other doors that admit you briefly to another world. From private gardens to quirky museums, woodland walks to seaside resorts, all of Great Britain is a treasure-house for the thoughtful and observant tourist. When you work hard as your own travel agent, you will eventually find yourself carrying a set of just the right keys.

A FEW FLOATING FACTS

Using a telephone? When calling from the United States to England (listed as "the United Kingdom" or "U.K." in most directories), you do not need to dial the 0 prefix given for U.K. numbers. But if you are calling within the U.K., you do need to use the 0 prefix. The country code for England is 44.

The British Tourist Authority is located at 551 Fifth Avenue, Suite 701, New York, NY 10176, telephone (212) 986-2200. It also has offices in Atlanta, Chicago, and Los Angeles. The toll-free number for the B.T.A. is (800) 462-2748.

BritRail's British Travel Shop sells Ordnance Survey maps and a wide range of other maps and guidebooks. Their address is 1500 Broadway, 10th floor, New York, NY 10036. Telephone orders can be placed at (212) 575-2667.

In England, the English Tourist Board, at Bromells Road, Clapham, London SW4 OBJ, can provide a directory of more than five hundred Tourist Information Centres throughout

Great Britain. Many of the publications of the English Tourist Board are available through the British Travel Bookshop (see above).

The National Trust's address for inquiries is P.O. Box 39, Bromley, Kent BRI 3XL, telephone 0181-464-1111. Their *mail order* address for a Holiday Cottage Brochure, £1 in 1995, is: Holiday Booking Office, P.O. Box 536, Melksham, Wiltshire SN12 8SX.

The Royal Oak Foundation, which is the U.S. affiliate of the National Trust, has offices at 285 West Broadway, New York, NY 10013. Their telephone is (212) 966-6565. Membership in the National Trust/Royal Oak also gives free admission to National Trust properties in Wales, Northern Ireland, and the National Trust of Scotland. A family membership in 1996 cost $65, an individual membership $40.

The National Trust for Scotland is at 5 Charlotte Square, Edinburgh, EH2 4DU.

The Landmark Trust is located at Shottesbrooke, Maidenhead, Berkshire SL6 3SW. Its telephone is 01628-825925, its fax 01628-825417. Its American branch is: The Landmark Trust, 28 Birge Street, Brattleboro, VT 05301. The telephone number for the Vermont office is (802) 254-6868.

Consumer Reports Travel Letter, which is published by Consumers Union, accepts no advertising. It is published monthly; in 1994, a year's subscription cost $39. Phone orders: (800) 234-1970, or write CRTL, Box 53629, Boulder CO 80322-3629.

Hotel discount programs vary a great deal in scope, cost of joining, and target audience. See the annual evaluation of these programs in *Consumer Reports Travel Letter* for details (back issues can be ordered from the address above). We have used *Entertainment Halfprice Europe*, which in 1995 cost $53 a year (toll-free order by telephone, (800) 285-5525), and ITC-50, under $40 a year (toll-free order by telephone, (800) 342-0558).

The Ordnance Survey is located at Romsey Road, Maybush, Southampton SO9 4DH. Its telephone line for information and public relations is 01703-792608. Its line for order processing is 01703-792910. (It is, of course, far handier to order these maps from an American address, but they may be able to tell you where to find your nearest outlet, or *stockist*.)

2

Draw Me a Map!

If I had to limit myself in my travels to just one small bag, most of it would probably be filled with maps. This chapter explains why.

When I think of England, I sometimes picture its familiar landscapes: seacoast, moors, rolling hills, hedgerows, sunken country lanes. But almost as often I see instead an infinitely detailed close-up, a rectangle covered with lines, symbols, and tiny print. These are mesmerizing hieroglyphics I have studied so intensely that after a long day on English roads or paths, they can drift before my eyes as I fall asleep. Nowhere but in England do I dream of maps.

Of course I use ordinary maps at home, the standard highway issue for trips into neighboring states and city street maps for locating unfamiliar addresses in Minneapolis and St. Paul. But useful as these maps are, they seem dull, unimaginative, and limited compared to the imposing splendor of England's Ordnance Survey series. These are distinctly royal maps. Each, in fact, carries a discreet notation: *Made and published by Ordnance Survey, Southampton. Crown copyright.*

This royal family of maps has its own definite hierarchy.

Reliable but unexciting, rather like two take-charge aunts in woolly cardigans and thick-soled brogues, the Road Atlas, set at the scale of one inch to four miles, and the Motoring Atlas, at a slightly larger 1:3, span the entire country. Together with the folding Routeplanner, telescoped to an efficient 1:10 for planning long-distance journeys, these atlases are all many motorists may think they need.

But anyone who wants to explore England in depth must make the acquaintance of the Routemaster series. With nine area sheets, the Routemaster (1:4) not only outlines major and minor roads but also indicates basic topography (woods, buildings, canals, lakes, marshes) and several other selected features, like antiquities (native fortress, site of battle, Roman road) and tourist information. The latter category is dizzyingly inclusive: abbeys, cathedrals and priories; aquariums; camp and trailer (British *caravan*) sites; castles; caves; country parks; craft centers; gardens; golf courses; historic houses; information centers; motor racing museums; nature trails; picnic sites; preserved railways; racecourses; skiing; viewpoints; wildlife parks; youth hostels; zoos. Ever helpful, the Routemaster also lists the frequencies for both regional BBC and independent radio, telephone numbers for weather forecasts, and road information.

At a scale of one inch to four miles, however, the Routemaster is not a map to pore over easily in a moving car, or at night with tired eyes under a weak hotel bulb. The next step up is the Tourist Map, part of a set ranging from one-half inch to one-and-a-quarter inch per mile and covering Nevis and Glen Coe, Dartmoor, Exmoor, Lake District, Loch Lomond and the Trossachs, New Forest, North York Moors, Peak District, Cotswolds, the Broads, Snowdonia and Anglesey.

Thinner than the Tourist Map, and with more sharply focused eyes, the Landranger sweeps over England with more
than two hundred maps at about one-and-a-quarter inch per
mile.

With the Tourist and Landranger series, the Ordnance
Survey really begins to hit its stride. These maps not only outline several varieties of roads, footpaths, and bridleways, but
they also deftly sketch in woods; orchards; bracken, heath, and
rough grassland; open pits; quarries; parks and ornamental
grounds. Besides greenhouses (British glasshouses), tollgates,
wind pumps, and entrances to tunnels, the Tourist Maps include weirs, fords, locks, beacons, dunes, flat rocks, cliffs,
slopes, shores of sand and shingle, and (note the distinction)
shores of sand and mud. The related Landranger boasts more
than one hundred similar types of topographic detail.

In these maps, the Ordnance Survey's masterly graphic
symbols observe fine discriminations: a windmill in use has
streaks of light shining from it, a disused windmill does not. A
sleight-of-hand adjustment carefully differentiates a church
or chapel with a tower (square with cross on top), from one
with a spire (circle with cross), or one without either (a plain
cross.) The Tourist Map neatly initials every post office, telephone booth (British call box), public house, club house, mile-
post, milestone, and town hall or equivalent. In rural areas, it
also courteously shows the way to the nearest public convenience (toilet).

With all these refinements, the Ordnance Survey does not
forget to convey fundamental topography. The Tourist Map is
shaded to indicate relief (varying height above sea level) in a
pale, pleasing spectrum from light green to blue-gray. The
Landranger, indulging in a somewhat brighter palette, also

boldly strokes in bright blue motorways, dark red trunk roads, yellow country lanes, dotted red footpaths, and dotted black plain paths. Since England is crisscrossed with footpaths, every large-scale Ordnance Survey map is covered with their squiggles. From a short distance, these maps look like a lifetime's labor from a painstakingly minute abstract painter who is equally adept at manipulating line and color.

As I gaze at these marvelous maps, admiring not only their intricate detail but also their artistry, something extraordinary often begins to happen. I feel as if I am slowly moving away from the countryside I am studying, ascending as if in a gently rising balloon high above the surface of the earth. Looking down, I suddenly have a unifying view of this particular section of England. I see, if only for a moment, not only how everything fits together but also how indescribably rich and layered the landscape is. I feel briefly kin to the awed American astronauts who reported seeing Earth in a new and humbling way.

But the Pathfinder and Outdoor Leisure Maps always bring me firmly and sensibly down to earth. Drawn at a very generous scale of two-and-a-half inches to one mile, these maps—virtual siblings—are intended for walkers and climbers, though motorists who plan to leave their cars even for short strolls off the road will also find them invaluable. With its additional markings of tourist attractions, Outdoor Leisure is slightly gaudier than the more serious Pathfinder.

The Pathfinder is indisputably the quintessential hiker's map. On any long distance footpath one sees veteran ramblers whose Pathfinders hang in waterproof plastic cases around their necks. What is the name of the next farm? That low hill? This small reservoir? Where is the mountain rescue telephone? The boundary of this field? Where does the fenced footpath become unfenced? Is this the marsh we're looking for? Shouldn't this patch of reeds be marked on the map? Where *are* we, anyway? The Pathfinder always knows.

Until I have looked at a Pathfinder or Outdoor Leisure Map or even Tourist Map of an area of England, I do not feel I have really been there. Collecting these maps has become a mild obsession. Others may gather postcards; I hoard maps. Some I order in advance by mail, but mostly I stop on the spot in England and search through the bookstores for the local specialties. Once, even though we were staying only two nights in the Brecon Beacons, I insisted on searching out the relevant Landranger. "Six dollars for a map for forty-eight hours?" queried James mildly. But he was glad the next day when I nosed out a footpath just off our main road that led to a spectacular view atop an easily accessible low mountain.

Just as other collectors often find their original focus extending to adjoining fields—from, say, salt-and-pepper pigs to pottery pigs to stuffed-animal pigs—so I also have extended the borders of my map mania. Not only do I love the Ordnance Survey, I also have a deep affinity for Geographers' A–Z, whose handy folding map of London cheered and guided me through my first visit to the city in 1960. The A–Z collection now includes atlases, road and county maps, town maps and street plans. A–Z can help a visitor thread through towns as diverse as Bath, Norwich, Oxford, and Stratford-upon-Avon, and as untouristy as Croydon, Reading, Swindon, and Wolverhampton.

Among my growing A–Z collection, Kent to Cornwall Holiday Map, set at five miles to an inch, is my favorite West Country trip planner. Its notations cheerfully range from well-known sites like Stonehenge or Glastonbury Abbey to such oddities as the Long Man, a standing stone near Eastbourne; Chesil Beach, a fifteen-mile bank of graded pebbles in Dorset; and the Museum of Mechanical Music at Goldsithney, Cornwall. A–Z's Kent County, at two-and-a-half miles per inch, is particularly useful to an aficionado of English gardens, since it locates not only the famous ones like Sissinghurst and Great Dixter, but lesser-known delights like Owl House Gardens, near Lamberhurst.

With their large black lettering, jazzy colors, and a general air of simplicity, most A–Z maps have a disarmingly popular appeal. "See?" the A–Z seems to say, encouragingly. "Reading this map isn't so difficult!"

But for sheer class, with a distinct whiff of English superiority, I always return to the Ordnance Survey. Safeway may be replacing the local greengrocer and butcher; Happy Chef looms on the motorway; malls are creeping into the countryside. But the Ordnance Survey can surely absorb such innovations and, perhaps, even put them firmly in their place—on a map.

A FEW FLOATING FACTS

Remember to omit the prefix "0" from an English telephone number when calling from the United States.

Some of these maps are available from the British Travel Bookshop, 551 Fifth Avenue, Suite 702, New York, NY 10176.

Ordnance Survey maps are stocked in many English bookstores. A list of American sources can be obtained from Public

Enquiries, Ordnance Survey, Romsey Road, Maybush, Southampton SO9 4DH. The telephone is 01703-792763, and the fax number is 01703-792888.

Besides Geographers A-Z Maps, look for Estate Publications Leisure Maps and Bartholomew Touring Maps, all available in many bookstores.

3

First-Class Illusion: Traveling Coach

Friends sometimes ask me, "How do you survive those awful all-night flights?" If I knew an easier and cheaper way to get to England, I'd take it. But until that time comes, this is how I cope.

When I fly, I always travel coach. Coach is, of course, the upscale word airlines prefer to economy, which is itself these days something of a misnomer. But so far I have resisted the blatant antagonism of a friend who calls it "cattle class." A descriptive term, I admit, and perhaps increasingly accurate. According to a recent consumer's travel newsletter, major airlines are continuing to reduce the width and leg room of coach seats. If a highly respectable health magazine is to be believed, pilots have now been instructed to save fuel by cutting down on the fan-fed flow of fresh air into the economy cabins. That's why, the magazine says, some passengers get sick.

Having a mind that seizes upon images, I have thought about my friend's term. Now when the gate attendant intones, "Please proceed to the door of Gate Six and have your boarding pass ready . . . ," an unsettling picture sometimes flashes before me. As we all dutifully rise, hoist carry-ons, and surge forward, I suddenly imagine our straggling line transformed. Arms rigidly at our sides, we march in close formation to the loading dock. Once inside the door, taken in charge by the flight crew, we are sorted and packed, each to his or her own tight slot. When the carton is filled, we take off. Not cattle, exactly, but perhaps cigars, chocolates, or anchovies. Or, in coach class, slightly cracked hard-boiled eggs.

But of course I have no intention of giving up flying, even if I have to remain part of an unwieldy sandwich. Nor do I want to sink into a passive acceptance of a second-class slot in life. So I have worked hard to turn my imagination in another direction, toward the illusion that, in fact, I am actually traveling first-class.

First, I make myself comfortable. (When I glimpse first-class passengers through an occasional drawn-back curtain, they certainly *look* comfortable.) If I were sitting up front, everyone would *know* I had pots of money, and I would not have to dress as if I did. So I wear loose, casual clothes: cotton slacks with an elastic or drawstring waist, a roomy overshirt, socks, and running shoes. In my carry-on I tuck a pair of folding slippers—which I wriggle into as soon as I sit down—and a sweater, just in case the cabin is *not* overheated and stuffy.

Ah, my carry-on: That is the secret of first-class success. It holds many other essentials. My half-size down pillow, for example, *and* a down neckroll pillow. The former I will use later as a bedpillow, and the latter on trips in our rented car. But on the plane, they combine to cushion my surprisingly bony edges when I curl up for a few hours' transatlantic snooze. Those small flat airline pillows do not, alas, cushion anything.

I often catch my seatmate looking at me surreptitiously as I unpack my carry-on. He or she is usually too polite to comment, but I can guess: "Have I got a certifiable nutcase here? And what do I do if she gets chatty?" Slippers, pillows, Walkman, tapes, books, magazines, sleep mask, earplugs, rubberized squeezable water bottle—out they come, to be stuffed into my bulging seat-pocket.

My beloved bright blue water bottle arouses the most curious glances. Since the air on board a plane is, I am told, as dry as the Sahara, it is a good idea to drink lots of water. But how often can one stand to crawl or climb over two other passengers to get to the aisle, which is probably clogged by a food cart anyway? So I bring my own water supply. If I wake in the night and am thirsty, I take a swig. I can't help that my water bottle looks rather like an updated wineskin and that when I drink, I have to tilt my head and squirt.

I will *not* get chatty. Some years ago, a professional geographer explained to me how city dwellers survive psychically. Most important, he said, is how they pretend they are isolated in an invisible cell of space on the subway or in the elevator or in line at the ticket office. They stare into the distance and refuse to make eye contact. I am something like a city dweller on an airplane. I want to disappear into my own private space (first class, with lots of room) and remain suspended there.

So I turn on my Walkman. This habit began during an uncomfortable period when I realized what Erica Jong meant about fear of flying. I found that listening to hypnotic music helped. Now I am addicted: As soon as I fasten my seat belt, I slip in one of my traveling tapes, quite different from my usual musical tastes. At twenty thousand feet, I depend on Kitaro, Steve Halpern, Crimson, the Celtic harp—the same tapes I take to the dentist, much to his gentle disdain, for he is a cultured man who sent one daughter to Juilliard and another to years of piano lessons. "No, I'm not listening to Mozart," I tell him. "It's airplane music." As the plane takes off, I sail away on soothing melodies. Over and over again the same tape plays, lulling me into a daze in which I forget I am sitting in an enclosed metal tube miles above the earth with nothing between me and sudden death but clouds.

After a while I may take out a book or leaf through a magazine. I choose my airplane reading carefully too. I avoid anything difficult, depressing, or experimental. I want either to be mesmerized, caught up in a fast-moving and well-written tale I can't put down, or else I want to read something so meditative, so full of insight that I can read just a few paragraphs, pause, and look out into the clouds to think for a while. I hope Thomas Merton would be wryly amused to find his *Conjectures of a Guilty Bystander* crammed into my carry-on next to the latest Tony Hillerman. Although I seldom read murder mysteries on the ground, I fervently wish Mr. Hillerman wrote one for every plane trip. When I am immersed either in Merton's speculations or in Hillerman's Navajo world, I am definitely in first class.

If I am flying at night across the ocean, I put my book away not long after takeoff, set my watch ahead to some ghastly hour next morning, and prepare to sleep. My seatmate may look at me oddly again. "What is she going to do about dinner? Isn't she going to watch the movie?" Because I do not travel well after a sleepless night, I have learned to zonk out early. In the airport before boarding, I always eat a packed home-cooked picnic supper—usually much tastier than airline food anyway. Drinks? Duty-free shopping? Forget it. With eye mask and earplugs, I don't even notice the movie.

Next morning, I open my carry-on again. Since I won't eat

lunch for some hours, and I need more than a roll and juice to keep me going, I have packed a breakfast supplement: a hard-boiled egg or piece of cheese or vanilla yogurt, a sourdough roll, green grapes, or a banana. Perhaps in first class, they're having eggs Benedict, but I wouldn't want all that extra fat. Since coach serves only lukewarm instant decaf, never brewed, I proffer my large plastic mug to the attendant and ask for plenty of hot water to steep my peppermint herbal tea bags.

After the morning tray of hot facecloths comes around, I freshen up with a few first-class touches: a slosh of hand lotion from my purse-size container (all that dry air) and a dab of perfume (sheer morale). Of course I have packed a tooth-brush. Then, since everyone else in the cabin seems to be stretching and walking around, I do too. In fact, during day flights I try to get up occasionally and hike the aisles, which gives me, at least temporarily, the illusion of room to move. I stroll purposefully, as if I were going to talk to someone at the back of the plane, and ignore both the stares of seated passengers and the sighs of flight attendants, who probably just wish we would all stay where we'd been packed.

As we file out of the plane, I see ahead of me the first-class passengers, who naturally leave first. But, I think nastily to myself, their bags won't arrive at the baggage-claim carousel any faster than mine. In fact, I really don't envy them as much this morning as I did last night, when I first pulled on my slippers and contorted myself into a shrinking fetal position.

Our flight over, I think about all the money those posh passengers spent for a few hours of extra-wide seats, hors d'oeuvres, champagne, and their very own flight attendant. Now it's all gone, with nothing to show for it. My whole vacation, how-

ever, is still ahead. First class, executive, business, coach—
what does it matter? Once I get the crick out of my back, my
legs loosen up, and I no longer hear a recurring refrain from a
New Age version of "Greensleeves," I'll just tell myself I traveled behind the curtain practically all the way.

4

The Joys of Eating In

When we mention travel plans to friends, most assume we're mainly going to eat. "Oh, if you're going to London, you can eat your way to heaven!" recently rhapsodized a self-proclaimed gourmand, launching into a recital of expensive temples of nouvelle cuisine, whose elaborate rituals we knew would take an entire evening. Most upscale travel guidebooks emphasize the delights of dining out, especially in four-star restaurants where the wine list is exquisite and the prices dazzling as well.

Even in my favorite budget handbooks, food plays an important role—understandably, for everyone has to eat. Since we do like good food, for years James and I dutifully bent our itineraries to include many recommended restaurants. We wandered around strange cities, took wrong turns, and sometimes arrived at an elusive quarry only to find an empty storefront or newly converted pizza parlor. We had been brainwashed by the conventional wisdom that part of the fun of traveling is always eating out.

But we are no longer believers. Now we listen to our friends politely, take a few notes to show appreciation, and tuck the restaurant lists under traveler's checks receipts, which we also hope we'll never need. After many trips coping with the mixed difficulty and pleasure of eating out, we have simplified our lives. We eat in.

On a recent trip to London, I said dreamily to James, "For lunch today I'd just like a large salad, with mixed greens, ripe avocado, sliced orange, a sprinkling of ricotta cheese, and a raspberry vinaigrette dressing. With a hot whole wheat roll on the side, and Greek yogurt topped by green grapes and raspberries for dessert. Of course, we deserve a private dining room, and I plan to wear jeans."

"I want broiled salmon with buttered boiled potatoes. And since it's actually sunny today, I insist on eating outside," my husband added. Then I scooped up a forkful of fresh crisp lettuce leaves, James dug into his perfectly cooked salmon, and we grinned at each other. As we lunched at a table on the back terrace of our London flat, we were congratulating ourselves on once again having our own kitchen.

We were converted one summer after a week of constant theatergoing in London, when we realized that we often needed to eat at hours good restaurants didn't want to serve us. Far too tired for a fashionable late dinner after a performance, we wished instead to eat a light supper at six P.M. in order to make a seven-thirty or eight o'clock curtain. But timing such a maneuver was difficult. Few restaurants opened that early, and service was unpredictable, sometimes so slow as to make us check our watches nervously, or so rapid as to leave us walking up and down the block outside the theater, watching for the doors to open.

Mornings weren't so easy either. Early risers who respectively like to walk and jog, we found an English breakfast at eight-thirty an excruciating wait. In other parts of the world, except in big hotels and in a few all-night American cafés, no one welcomed us at six or seven A.M.

Even when we could find restaurants willing to feed us at odd hours, we didn't always like what they offered. Though we are both practiced cooks, we prefer understated meals—broiled fish or roasted chicken, steamed vegetables with herbs, pasta with a simple sauce. At home I'm a semivegetarian. Our querulous stomachs rebelled after night upon night of veal marsala, blackened redfish, roulades of beef with wine sauce, or cheesy omelettes melting in a pool of delicious but disastrous butter.

If one of us was temporarily laid up with headache or cold, we daydreamed aloud about a boiled egg or a bowl of hot soup or a single piece of toast with honey. Although room service might bring cold toast, it could cost almost as much as an ordinary meal eaten in the hotel dining room.

Eating out in general costs lots of money. Raised in thrifty Iowa, I would try not to think, on a typical evening out, as I looked at James's plate of lamb chops, potatoes, and peas, how I could easily make that at home for about $4, though here in a mediocre restaurant we were paying $30. And I'd reluctantly left Liberty's that afternoon without a new silk scarf because, even at their summer sale, it was still too expensive.

So we began looking on our trips for rooms with kitchens, or at least with hot plates and refrigerators, as well as furnished flats and cottages. We don't usually bother for short stays of a night or two, and of course we still eat out for some meals. But now eating out is a high occasion rather than a necessity.

Eating in has many advantages. Shopping for food, we meet local people. Hunting for fish in the Mayfair section of

London, I have chatted with both aristocratic shoppers and a friendly fishmonger who invited me to watch him prepare a whole poached salmon on a silver platter. Especially in smaller towns, fellow shoppers graciously advise me on how to distinguish among varieties of potatoes. They then often ask about our travel plans, our American home, and whether we know so-and-so in Chicago.

We eat elegantly when we eat in—the freshest of fish, meat, and produce. In London we've had delicious pastries, brioches, and lemon curd from a nearby Justin de Blank bakery; an astonishing variety of yogurts and cheeses from a Safeway near the Barbican; dense dark bread freshly baked in Crank's; and minced beef ground before our eyes by a neighborhood butcher. In the countryside we've feasted on local apples, strawberries, and raspberries, as well as tender langoustines— tastier than lobster—caught that same day near Gairloch, the town in the Scottish Western Highlands where we were staying.

To make cooking as easy as possible, we stick to simple dishes—bake, boil, broil, or fry, and serve. No fuss, very little cleanup. A dinner of, say, broiled fish, baked potato, and salad, usually takes us less time to prepare than if we'd sat in a restaurant, waited for a menu, waited again to order, and waited even longer to be served. (While we eat, we can also indulge ourselves, if we wish, in a little gin rummy, as part of our fiercely competitive lifetime series. Can you see us dealing out cards while eating in a respectable restaurant?)

Once I calculate what we save, suites with kitchens or flats and cottages—usually rented only by the week, however—are surprisingly reasonable. Even if an English hotel provides breakfast, and these days not every one does, it is hard to eat lunch and dinner out without tossing away at least an addi-

tional $50 to $75 for two per day, probably more. And that figure doesn't allow for any snacks, appetizers, wine, or fancy
desserts. (Try pricing fresh berries and clotted cream in a good
restaurant.)

But eating in saves more than money. It saves temper,
hunger pangs, and energy. When we return from a trip these
days and friends eagerly ask us about what great restaurants
we discovered, they look disappointed when we tell them:
"No great restaurants. But great food!"

They don't really want to hear about sautéed fresh fillet of
hake with butter and lemon juice, or tiny new English potatoes tossed with parsley and snipped cress, or those fragrant,
juicy strawberries we bought at a roadside stand and devoured with thick Devon cream. So we keep quiet.

But on a four-star chart, I privately give five to our kitchens
away from home.

A FEW FLOATING FACTS

Renting the kind of place where you have your own kitchen is
called in England *self-catering*. For information on different
types of self-catering accommodation, see Chapter One, "How
to Be Your Own Travel Agent."

5

In Praise of Overpacking

"Are *all* these bags yours?" asks the taxi driver, looking critically at the heap next to the curb. "Yes," I say, trying not to sound apologetic. But as I climb into the backseat, clutching my carry-on, I wonder a little resentfully if he would ask Elizabeth Taylor the same question. I've read with self-justifying relief about how *she* travels.

James pops into the backseat beside me. "Got everything?" he asks cheerfully, knowing I will have compulsively counted: his duffel bag, my Pullman-on-wheels, the spare folding suitcase for souvenirs and purchases, the tote bag of cooking supplies for our kitchen-equipped cottage, his carry-on, my carry-on, the portable computer, and my bottomless shoulder bag.

This is not how I used to travel. When I was much younger, I studied helpful articles in newspapers and magazines with titles like "An Insider's Travel Tips" or "A Celebrated Jet-Setter Tells How to Pack for Your Trip." I absorbed the one unshakable rule: Virtue lies in traveling light. My sophistication as well as personal morality, I learned, were sure to increase as the size and weight of my suitcase went down. Although the matched set of Samsonite luggage I'd been given on graduation from high school was still good—in fact, its heavy plastic-molded cases were practically indestructible—it was definitely not what anyone would now call politically correct.

So I began a long search for the Perfect Bag. It would be sturdy, infinitely expandable, affordable—and ultra lightweight. In luggage departments of various stores, I would find myself scientifically weighing one suitcase against another. Not only pounds, but ounces became crucial. Clerks, who obligingly provided either scales or statistical information, acted as my lab assistants. Like the four-minute mile, the ten-pound suitcase became a goal that seemed impossible to surpass. But some manufacturer did, and then I raised my standards again. Could I find a replacement that weighed seven pounds? Five? Two?

When I'd settled on the lightest possible suitcase (which, however, seemed to grow unaccountably heavy as soon as it was filled), I would worry about how to pack. Of course I knew about travel-size toiletries, folding toothbrushes, and raincoats that fit into their own pockets. But how else could I conserve? "Pack what you think you'll need, and then take out half of that!" my media advisers warned me. One pair of pajamas, a windproof jacket, a hat, a dress, slacks, a warm sweater, one turtleneck, a shirt, walking shoes, dress-up shoes, and minimal underwear almost filled up my space—and I hadn't yet allowed for a single change of clothes, or a small hair dryer, or a book to read at night. Was I supposed to limit myself to half a pair of pajamas, or maybe half the book?

"Wear your slip to bed at night and you won't need pajamas," continued my coaches, who were full of practical if often supercilious hints. "Toss your raincoat over your slip if you have to walk through a hall to the bathroom. This will save packing a bathrobe."

I think it was the canard about raincoats that finally decided me. One cold, rainy evening in England, when I clambered out of a tub in a large unheated bathroom and shivered as I quickly toweled off with a thin, worn square ("Never waste space on towels!"), I reached for my all-purpose raincoat. It was still damp from the downpour whose effects I had hoped to dispel with a hot bath. Slipping my arms into its clammy sleeves and pulling on my soaked shoes ("You can certainly get along without bedroom slippers!"), I vowed as I fled to my room that I would begin compromising my virtue for a modicum of comfort.

My descent into depravity was gradual but complete. Now when I travel, I take whatever I think I may need, and although my suitcases (plural) are heavier, my spirits are much lighter. Because I sometimes pad down drafty halls in the middle of the night, I pack warm slippers—and a lightweight but comfortable robe, just dandy for a quick nap or rainy-day lounging or breakfast in bed. I tuck in other essentials: camera, extra film, rain hat, head scarf for windy days, sunglasses, suntan lotion, a miniature FM radio, herbal teabags, a large plastic mug for airliner coffee, several unread *New Yorkers*, scissors, transparent tape, waterproof boots, a plastic bag of detergent, a small sewing kit, address book, pocket packs of facial tissue, a washcloth, a small hand towel, a first aid kit including safety pins and Band-Aids, pads of paper and pens, a deck of cards, and a Thermos.

Each of these items (and others I haven't listed, lest I be reported to the P. C. travel police) has proved its worth. When an essential folding map rips along its well-used lines halfway through a trip, I can produce the saving tape. A deck of cards turns a six-hour delayed takeoff into a marathon gin-rummy contest. Handing my giant-size mug to the flight attendant, I don't have to wait forever until she is back to dispense my next three ounces.

My new golden rule of travel is: DON'T WASTE TIME AND MONEY LOOKING FOR IT ABROAD IF YOU CAN POSSIBLY TAKE IT WITH YOU. One noted travel columnist counseled recently: "If in doubt, don't pack it. Remember you can buy it there." Ah, but has she tried finding a shop that sells Band-Aids—or shampoo, or eyeglass pins, or a computer disc—in a tiny French village on a Sunday afternoon? Or spending several long evenings in a remote Italian hilltop cottage with nothing to read? Or forking over four times the ordinary cost of a roll of film to an airport extortionist?

I am also puzzled by those fashion writers who extol the six-piece interchangeable all-purpose wardrobe plan. How do they feel, personally, about wearing the same black jersey dress for fourteen consecutive nights, even if they are allowed to add a dashing scarf or a string of faux pearls? I, personally, want to take a pair of tongs and drop that dress in the nearest dustbin. As for the common recommendation of casually tossing a cashmere cardigan over designer jeans, the price of that little outfit would probably edge out my airfare to London.

So I return, somewhat doggedly, to my old staples: an extra pair of baggy slacks, for instance, so I'll have something to wear tomorrow if I slip in a muddy patch today, silk long-johns for those cold nights when the hotel's nylon blanket just isn't enough, a bright red turtleneck for the days I can't face yet again putting on the green one. Most of my separates match, but if I feel wonderful in a shocking pink silk shirt, I don't worry if it doesn't go with anything except one skirt. I pack it away. Life is short.

I even pack my pillow. When we arrive at our hotel, I plump it on the bed and know I won't wake up with a cranky neck from one of those extra-firm semibolsters. I have become quite fond of my little pillow, rather as a child might travel with a comforting teddy bear.

This sort of pack-it-all philosophy is possible only, of course, with a certain kind of itinerary. When I was twenty, I hitchhiked around England with a backpack, itself a mandate for minimalism. Now James and I usually fly to a city and stay in a hotel, or we rent a car at the airport and head off to the countryside, where we also usually pick one spot and stay there for a week or two. Neither plan involves much transfer of luggage. We seldom have to drag our bags very far. Airports have rental carts and skycaps; most hotels have bellhops.

Admittedly, I still look with concealed admiration at the woman who strides off the plane with only a garment bag and a raincoat (also her bathrobe?) over her arm. But I wonder how she'll feel if she has to walk around in her slip every night and stand in her bare feet on icy tile floors. Might she catch cold? And if so, does she by chance have any decongestant, aspirin, and rosehip tea?

6

⚜

A Supermarket of
Souvenirs

Searching for affordable souvenirs in England is not always easy. Friends and relatives often expect something, but what? Even with the pound devalued, cashmere sweaters are still stunningly expensive, and a skirt length of Harris tweed or Scotch tartan might, for a cost-conscious tourist, involve giving up a long-awaited tea at the Dorchester. (And who do you know who wants a tartan skirt?) Most of the fairly inexpensive trinkets at street stands—little soldiers in tall fur hats, miniature British flags, dish towels illustrating the Tower of London, smart-alecky T-shirts—are either flimsy or gaudy, or both. So what can a traveler on a limited budget find?

Plenty—if that traveler can stop eyeing the quaint pseudo-Tudor storefront of Liberty's and look instead for a mundane but well-stocked supermarket: Sainsbury, Safeway, Gateway, Tesco, Waitrose, or Asda, among others. Although both London and country towns still abound in small shops, the fruiterer, butcher, and baker (not to mention the candlestick maker) are hard pressed by American-style chains, some so ambitious they include even hardware sections, fast food counters, and children's play areas.

Inside these emporia of food and drink, and in some smaller grocery stores, a souvenir hunter can quickly fill a cart with distinctive reminders of England that cost only a few dollars or less. Since many American supermarkets (and specialty shops in metropolitan areas) carry selected English imports—After Eight mints, for example, Carr's Water Biscuits, Twining's Earl Grey tea, or Baxter's orange marmalade—I avoid such obvious choices. Many other possibilities await, however, including less ordinary variations on familiar themes: Dundee Three-Fruit Marmalade (orange, lemon, and grapefruit), for under $2, or Hovis Butter Puffs, or Mint Humbugs, both for less than $1.

Certain sections of the supermarket provide better hunting grounds than others. Despite the tempting array of cheeses, fancy yogurts, and other creamy concoctions, I am wary of anything perishable. Stilton once perfumed my carry-on for weeks after arrival, and U.S. Customs looks askance at fresh produce. Instead, I head for the aisles that cater to certain benign English addictions.

Take *biscuits* (cookies to an American) and crackers. I always do: several boxes of them, long-lasting, lightweight, eminently packable. The English have to eat something with their tea. What ingenuity Americans expend on an endless array of frozen foods, the English devote to their biscuits and crackers.

In the new sprawling Sainsbury in East Grinstead, Sussex, about an hour outside London, I found shelves heaped with possibilities, including Hovis Crackers, a round wheat biscuit; McVitie's Cheddars, round and cheesy; Simmers MacVita, wholemeal crackers with bran; Jacob's Brown Wheat, "Original and Best," all priced from 65 cents to just over a dollar. Many of these crackers are practically gift-wrapped as souvenirs; Jacob's Choice Grain, made of kibbled wheat and rye, barley flakes and bran, has a shiny paper covering illustrated by a village scene and stamped impressively "By Appointment to Queen Elizabeth, the Queen Mother Biscuit Makers."

From an almost infinite cookie assortment, I singled out ginger thins, like ginger snaps; Highland Oatcakes, a flat, grainy circle of oatmeal, fat, wheat, sugar, and flour; and Milk Chocolate Rustics, an oatflake sweetened digestive biscuit priced as cheaply as crackers.

When I wheeled my cart around a corner and confronted the candy aisle, I stood for a moment in awe. This was a greedy child's dream: brightly colored sweets of all kinds in small transparent packages, almost piled to the ceiling. Even the names seemed tempting: "Cool Mint Crumbles," white hard candies; "Devon Toffees"; "Fruit Jellies," softer than "American Hard Gums"; "Sherbet Cocktails," hard candies in pastel tones, and, of course, "Turkish Delight," a critical ingredient in Dorothy Sayers's classic murder mystery, *Strong Poison*.

Of course, not every friend would appreciate a sugar high. Fortunately, my chosen Sainsbury offered intriguing alternatives. In selecting a supermarket souvenir, I always look carefully at packaging, preferring distinctive graphics, attractive colors, certifiably English illustrations, and, whenever possible, the reproduced royal warrant, that discreet printed notice of "By Appointment . . ." to Her Majesty, or to one of her near relatives. The soup aisle proved fruitful, quite literally, for Baxter's ("By Appointment to Her Majesty the Queen Fruit Canners," and evidently skilled at vegetables as well) offers a variety of canned soups, handsomely decorated, in flavor combinations that seemed peculiarly English: carrot and butter bean; butter bean and parsnip; and the grandest, royal game soup, with a stately picture of a stag on the front, and listed ingredients of Highland water, game, venison, pheasant, grouse, and vegetables.

A tiny round container of Patum Peperium ("The Gentleman's Relish, the Original 1828 Recipe"), from Eisenham Quality Foods, would need only a card to go with it. Patum Peperium's finely lettered black-on-white wrapper is crammed with information ("Anchovy Relish with Butter, Spices & Herbs, for toast, biscuits, savouries, canapes.") Though a little pricey, at about $2, the Gentleman's Relish looks gratifyingly upper class.

More plebeian but perhaps more authentically contemporary are the individual servings, packaged for "long life" (the food's, not the purchaser's), of steak and kidney pudding and spiced apple pudding. The problem for me was that both puddings looked identical, and I thought perhaps they tasted that way as well. I chose instead to load up on a favorite I can't find at home, a box of twelve genuine crumpets, for about fifty cents. Not at all the same as English muffins, these soggy little cakelike rounds toast to perfection and quickly soak up jam, resulting in a yummy treat that needs no added butter.

Jams, jellies, and marmalades rated a large section in my Sainsbury. Frank Cooper's Fine Cut Oxford Marmalade ("By Appointment to Her Majesty Marmalade Maker") was under two dollars, and individual jars of jam, so small the "By Appointment" royal crest was almost indecipherable, were a mere twenty-five cents each, in flavors like Wilkin & Sons' Morello Cherry, or Nelson's Bramble Seedless Conserve. A few such jars could be tucked into a basket or box with some Jacob's Choice Grain Crackers or a pack of crumpets. I grabbed one to eat with my hard roll on the long airplane trip home.

Candies, crackers, and jams are not the only supermarket index to the English national character. The English famously love their pets, and one long aisle in Sainsbury reflected that passion. I briefly considered some tasty souvenirs for my own two cats: Spiller's Purrfect Selection, a cat dinner of beef, liver, and rabbit, or another of chicken, salmon, and trout. Even when they ate food from a can rather than dry kibble, my deprived American cats never had a chance at rabbit, salmon, or trout.

If I had been shopping for a dog-owning friend, I could never have resisted Sainsbury's "Marrowbone Rolls." Not only did it sound juicily nutritious (no mere anonymous bones ground into these dog biscuits), but a lyrical picture on its package showed an undoubtedly English dog in a doghouse surrounded by English roses, with fields and a quaint village church in the background.

Other surprising souvenirs appeared in unlikely aisles. My Sainsbury, for example, sold large attractive vinyl *shoppers* (tote bags or carryalls to an American), bright green with an antique Sainsbury logo, for about seven dollars each. In the toiletries aisle, Sainsbury really came into its own, offering a variety of cosmetics and sundries under its own label, Nature's Compliments, whose logo was adorned with pastel English flowers. For sheer uniqueness as an English souvenir, I did not think I could surpass a compact oval container of lovage and celandine deodorant.

But I could not think of many friends to whom I'd dare risk giving deodorant as a souvenir, even if it was scented with genteel-sounding English herbs. I could more comfortably bestow bars of Wright's Coal Tar Soap. Its deliberately old-fashioned wrapper, done in sepia tones, showed a Victorian father with suspenders next to his two children. They were all lathering up together as the mother looked on approvingly. The label reassured potential customers that its soap, first made by William Valentine Wright in about 1860, "was different from other soaps, because it offered deep cleansing and antiseptic properties. Now, 130 years on, Wright's Coal Tar Soap has changed very little. It still retains its honest natural and thorough deep-cleansing appeal, and has been used by generations of families." History, tradition, and honesty, not to mention soap—all this for under seventy-five cents a bar. How could I go wrong?

Loaded with soap, deodorant, little jams, crackers, candies, relish, soup, and a capacious carryall to tote everything home, I happily walked out of the supermarket with change from a ten-pound and a five-pound note. Having spent less than $25 for an assortment of modest but authentic souvenirs, I now had only the problem all gift-laden returning travelers secretly face. Should I keep the royal game soup for a cold winter's day at home? Could I really bear to part with my Patum Peperium? Would anyone else possibly appreciate those mint humbugs as much as I would?

A FEW FLOATING FACTS

Prices of these souvenirs were estimated for a British pound at $1.60, and these prices may be somewhat higher (seldom lower!) by the time you read this—but still a bargain.

Sainsbury superstores can be found in central London, although not every branch carries the range of goods sold at the East Grinstead store. Even small deli and grocery stores, which abound almost everywhere in London, should provide a sampling of edible souvenirs.

7

How to Keep
a Travel Journal

*E*arly in the morning, before the crowds arrive, you enter Salisbury Cathedral. Someone is practicing Bach on the pipe organ, and its deep, joyous voice floats somewhere above as you slowly walk down the shadowy aisles. You are struck by the serenity of this medieval church, which has sheltered knights, squires, tradesmen and peasants, contemporaries of Shakespeare and of Dickens, soldiers leaving for World War I and II, and now those living at the troubled end of the twentieth century. Outside, sitting for a while in a sudden burst of sunshine on the vast green lawn of the cathedral close, you arch your neck until it hurts to admire Salisbury's graceful spire.

Wandering later through the market square, you stop for morning coffee in a bustling, warm tearoom, filled with the British accents of townspeople out shopping or visiting. When you politely ask the gray-haired woman behind the counter how to find the road to Stonehenge, she hears *your* accent and inquires where you are from. Astonishingly, she has a son who works for a university in your hometown.

Although Stonehenge is full of people filing past its fences, you are still moved by its mysterious solemnity. You are surprised by how lonely it seems, even surrounded by a cordoned fence and visitors, as it looms above the rolling Salisbury Plain. As you sit on a bit of ledge in the parking lot and eat a picnic lunch, sandwiches from the tearoom in Salisbury, you stare at the silent monoliths and wonder.

After lunch you try to follow a map to Heale House, a garden that seems very close but somehow keeps receding. Everyone in your car has an opinion about how to get there, but you still end up creeping down more country lanes than you could have imagined in one small square on the map. Finally you arrive, tired and cross, but you revive as you stretch out in the sun—yes, it is still shining!—on the banks of the Avon, a shallow, fast-moving stream that runs through the garden. You especially like the little red Oriental bridge that leads to a tiny island with a Japanese pagoda.

Late in the afternoon, you arrive at Stourhead, a park owned by the National Trust. With its carefully planned viewpoints, elegant architectural follies, and smooth, curving lake, you realize immediately why it is called the masterpiece of English landscape art. When you turn off the light that night in your room at the Spread Eagle Inn, just outside Stourhead, you turn to your companion and say, sleepily, "That was a great dinner tonight. I didn't realize shepherd's pie could taste so good. And what a wonderful day. I don't think I'll ever forget it."

But, alas, you do forget. A few months later you have trouble recalling details—not how beautiful Salisbury Cathedral was, but the sunshine on the green; not the charming garden with its red bridge, but what river flowed through it; not the cozy inn outside Stourhead, but its name, so you can recommend it to your friends who are leaving for England next week and who want to reserve a room. In fact, as you try to tell your England-bound friends where to go and what to do, you cannot reconstruct everything. Every day was so full, and you saw so much.

That is why I keep a travel journal. Although at the time I'm sure I'll remember it all, I usually don't. With a journal, I can quickly look up places and names, months or even years later. When I reread it aloud to my husband, we will instantly find ourselves back on the flat road through the Norfolk fenlands, or plashing on foot down a narrow muddy path near Ullswater, or sitting in a tiny dining room in a hotel in Portloe, Cornwall, where we contemplate a swimming dish of stewed chicken, so overcooked it has almost disintegrated.

A travel journal is the only kind I've ever been able to keep. Many times, goaded by other writers who advised me a daily journal was essential, I have tried. But I was always daunted by the dullness of my entries: "Lingering sore throat today. Can't get rid of this cold. Spent the morning at the vet's with Sheba, who evidently has a bad case of hair balls. Worked on book this afternoon, but too many phone calls. Didn't get much done." When I tried more profound statements, I usually felt awkward, and they always looked phony on paper.

But that, I discovered, is the beauty of a travel journal. It *should* be prosaic; for me, its value is in direct proportion to how specific its entries are. The quick jottings I make are simply intended to remind me of where I was on a particular day and what exactly I did. Once I recall where and what, my memory usually supplies the flavor and texture of my experience. Often the meaning of that experience becomes clearer after some time has passed. So, as I write in my travel journal,

I do not need to tell myself how important it is to say something significant. I can just make a few notes and go to bed.

Most of the difficulty of a travel journal is finding the time to do it. The time itself isn't much—as little as ten minutes, perhaps as much as a half hour, rarely more—but most days on our trips are both busy and tiring. It can take fierce discipline to keep up my journal. Sometimes I squeeze in a few moments before or after dinner, but on other days I am too depleted to face even a modest effort until the next morning. Then, after breakfast, realizing I don't dare let another day eclipse what happened on the day before, I pour myself a third cup of tea and settle at the dining room table with my notebook computer.

Although I did recently begin traveling with a computer, for many years I kept my travel journals with pen in a small, inexpensive, spiral notebook. (I advise buying such a notebook before departure in order not to waste time searching for one the first few days abroad.) Since a notebook fits handily into my purse, I always carry one on which to make quick notes in a garden, museum, restaurant, or theater.

So now you have a notebook and pen. What next? Besides your itinerary or schedule, I'd suggest just recording what seems either important or interesting (to *you*, not to your guidebook, or tour leader, or companions). *Interesting* is a very individual matter; so is *important*. Once, walking through a tiny Exmoor museum in Lynton, I smiled to see among its exhibits a dusty jar of homemade gooseberry jelly dated 1915. A note of that, I realized later, instantly brought back all the informality and homey feeling of the museum. I could easily imagine myself living in the little village of Lynton eighty years ago, putting up my fall store of gooseberry jelly. I am often transported to the past by an ordinary artifact of daily life—a child's dress, a featherbed, a frying pan.

When James and I once took an unexpected detour near Plaxtol, Kent, to Old Soar Manor, a partial ruin from about 1290, at first I had a hard time envisioning anyone living in its barren, swept spaces. But then I read the placard next to the *garderobe*, a small room opening off the main hall of the manor's private quarters. This closet, I learned, was both toilet and storage space. Waste dropped through the floor to the ground below, where it would be scooped out through an open archway. The resulting smell was supposed to prevent moths from damaging the clothes stored in the closet. Suddenly the crowded closeness, the huddled warmth, the stench of medieval life in that manor, came sharply into focus. Two lines in my journal still bring it back.

Journal notes can be quite short. If I were to make an entry for the day in and around Salisbury I outlined above, it might read something like this: "Salisbury. Absolutely wonderful! Someone playing Bach, music floats above. So serene. Sunshine all day! Sat outside for a while looking at spire. Coffee and delicious jam tarts in little tearoom in town. Met a woman whose son teaches statistics at the U. Then off to Stonehenge—crowded but impressive. Countryside around so lonely. Lunch (smoked salmon sandwiches from tearoom) in parking lot. Got lost trying to find Heale House garden; Doris in backseat kept giving wrong directions. Loved little red Oriental bridge. Stourhead—an hour's slow walk around lake, great trees, daffodils still blooming, also magnolias, azaleas, rhodos. Shepherd's pie at Spread Eagle Inn. Great day."

A scholarly reader may notice, with scrupulous alarm, that I have recorded very few actual facts about either Salisbury

Cathedral or Stourhead—their dates of completion, for example, designers, or history. Long ago I decided that any amount of money spent on brochures and guidebooks was a pittance compared to the other costs of an overseas trip. So rather than accumulating data in my notebook, I buy it ready-made for a pound or two.

I also supplement my travel journal with snapshots. Like local guidebooks, photographs are a sure way for me to evoke once more the sights and sensations of a trip. Loaded with film from my discount emporium at home, I snap with abandon: architecture, landscape, people. Some pictures—a weathered farm gate, an eighteenth-century balustrade, a pub sign, fallen magnolia petals on glistening green grass—are my own idiosyncratic views of the character of a place. Other pictures are just quick documentation. I'll nab on film an explanatory poster, identifying plaque, or memorial tablet, for example, rather than copy all its information into my notebook.

What I do try to put down are the details that capture my feeling about a place. Although I was fascinated by Cricket St. Thomas Wildlife Park in Dorset, a setting known to many American fans of imported British television as the background for *To the Manor Born*, I thought it was peculiar as well. My notebook entry says: "How odd it seemed to see Bactrian camels grazing in the Dorset fields—or, even more, a flock of improbable pink flamingos mixing with English ducks in the water."

I didn't bother to list all the animals in the park, but I wanted to retain one scene: "Best of all: the frolicking kids in the children's zoo, tussling with each other, gamboling. (I've never quite seen this before, an actual illustration of the word—the kids leap and seem to kick their heels together—

one kept jumping on his mother's back and trying to stay on for the ride.)" I always note the weather—in this case, "a chilly gray morning, and the trees are just starting to bud out"—and now, when I read my journal and picture Cricket St. Thomas, I see those gamboling lambs under a gray March sky. They lift my spirits with each leap.

Besides weather, I usually make quick notes about food. "Lunch at the Wind Whistle Pub, overpriced and typically English: I had a Stilton ploughman's garnished with creamy coleslaw, bits of lettuce and cress and tomato, and a thick brown chutney like shoe polish." In that entry, about a Dorset pub whose name my husband and I liked so much we stole it for our weekend cabin, I hear my own wry acceptance of English pub fare, which I've eaten so often that a ploughman's (a slab of cheese and a roll) is probably more familiar to me than a Big Mac.

Like American fast food, I eat pub food mostly because it is relatively quick and cheap. That doesn't mean I always like it. But, as my entry reminds me, I do appreciate the fresh garnishes—the plentiful leaves of English (that is, Boston) lettuce, the sharp little sprouts of cress, the surprisingly tasty greenish tomato—always more cheering than the faded radish and limp carrot sticks I might find on an inexpensive sandwich plate at home. Probably that day I washed it all down with a glass of sweet cider. Just rereading my entry (and now writing about it) makes me wish I were perched on a stool in that dark, warm pub, sipping cider and nibbling on those sprouts.

Sometimes an odd detail, something that doesn't seem related to anything, hovers in my mind until I write it down. When James and I explored Bedgebury Pinetum, a nature reserve in Kent dedicated to conifers, I noted: "We visited briefly at the shop (where I bought a new stick) with the ranger, who was accompanied by his two beautiful mixed-breed *lurchers*, dogs with soulful eyes and sleek bodies. Because they were white, Gypsies didn't want them—no good for poaching."

What that entry told me, I realized later, was how friendly the English usually are when you inquire about their animals. After describing how he'd rescued his dogs, the park *warden* (ranger to me) went on to talk with us about our impressions of the pinetum, our trip in general, our home state. He even helped me select a new walking stick from the small group bunched in an umbrella stand; inexpensive walking sticks are often sold in England in places where, at home, I'd expect to see T-shirts. From that note in my journal, I'll always know exactly where I got my favorite stick.

As for the lurchers themselves, I had never before seen these elegant animals, rather like greyhounds, with soft, gentle eyes. They lay quietly at their master's feet, sensitive to his every intonation, and he in turn clearly cherished them. Hearing that Gypsies had purportedly abandoned these dogs because their white coats made them too visible for poaching purposes, I was then forced to think, however briefly, about the tenuous survival of Gypsies in England—and the prejudices and stereotypes that surrounded them.

A quick image can sometimes fix the contradictions of a culture indelibly in memory—or, at least, in one's journal. One Sunday morning, as James and I were driving on the M25 outside London, a freeway jammed with racing traffic even on a weekend, I happened to look up to a high pedestrian overpass. There, with cars whizzing just below, a woman in full riding regalia, from helmet to jodhpurs, calmly paced her high-stepping horse across the roaring M25. I assumed she was heading for a bridle path somewhere on the other side. Grabbing my notebook from my purse, I wrote three words to remind me of the clash (or accommodation?) of English rural and urban life: "Horse on freeway!"

Besides evoking special moments, my travel journal also is useful for helping me avoid certain mistakes on our next trip. During our first stay at the Landmark Trust's Cloth Fair flat in London, I discovered, to my dismay in the middle of the night, that the church bells of St. Bartholomew the Great across the street rang every hour. *Every hour*: eleven, midnight, one A.M., two A.M., three A.M. At four o'clock I thankfully lost count. In the daytime the bells rang cheerily above the noisy, busy streets surrounding Smithfield Market, but at night they tolled a lament for loss of sleep. "Bells of St. Bart's: BRING EARPLUGS!" I wrote in caps. A year later, when we prepared to return to the same flat, I reread my journal, added earplugs to my packing list, and no longer had to sleep all week with a pillow over my head.

Some warnings to myself are more subtle, telling me not to let idyllic visions obscure certain realities. On an Easter Sunday when James and I attended a service in St. Paul's Cathedral, I'd been looking forward to hearing choral music in that grandest of spaces. But, as my notes remind me, the church was packed; we sat on folding chairs at the rear; I could not see what was going on, and, worse, all the music was disconcertingly piped out of a tinny loudspeaker just above my left ear. It was not an outstanding spiritual experience. Next time, either we'd go very, very early, or we might try another, less famous church.

Reading my journal entry about that Easter morning, I can

sense my irritation and fatigue. We'd arrived in London only the afternoon before, on a delayed flight, and I'd been struggling with a bad case of jet lag. My journal helps me remember how I actually *felt* from day to day. Just before we'd left, I'd had to cope with a last-minute bungled house repair, a broken alarm system, a sudden unexpected errand, and a raging headache (all dourly noted in my first entry). Unlike brochures, guidebooks, and even photographs, a journal doesn't let me pretend that everything on a trip is always wonderful.

So, looking back, I read: "Slept badly, hard to get out of bed. These first few days are always difficult." Or: "Very tired all day today." On another morning: "James got up at five A.M., and although I tried to stay in bed, I couldn't get back to sleep. I do wish he were the sort who could lie in bed and think, or doze." I find I'm quite a complainer, mentioning a slow start to the day, an overly late lunch, a too-long hike, unseasonably hot weather, a missing umbrella.

Yet these grumpy comments are almost always embedded in long entries about what I've noticed or enjoyed. So now when I'm having a bad day on a trip, I often think of my past travel journals. This too will pass, I tell myself, and something may yet happen today that is quite wonderful.

When evening comes, and I sit down with my journal, I always find the day held far more than I supposed: the delicious butterbrickly taste of Hokey Pokey, an ice cream I found in Porthleven, Cornwall; an empty medieval barn, cavernous but majestic, at Buckland Abbey, Devon; lights coming on at late dusk in far-flung farms across a Dorset valley; a handsome bearded gardener at Standen House who, on hearing that I too was an enthusiastic gardener, took time from his work to identify all the flowers I didn't know. Each of these moments added up to the final richness of our trip. I even treasure the apologetic answer of a worried hostess at a one-day benefit opening of Carclew Gardens in Cornwall when I inquired about a ladies' room: "Oh, I don't think toilets were advertised!"

So although my travel journal occasionally reveals damp days and damper spirits, lumpy beds, and disastrous meals, it (almost) never says "I wish I were home." When I open it again, weeks or months or years later, it has, in fact, the reverse effect. It makes me want to pack my bags, grab my maps, dash to the airport, catch the next plane to Gatwick, and start my trip all over again. Fortunately, thanks to my travel journal, I can.

II

The Thumbprint
Theory of Travel

A Note on the Thumbprint Theory
of Travel

I firmly subscribe to the thumbprint school of travel. This commits James and me to spending at least a week in one spot no larger than my thumbprint covers on a large-scale map of England. Excursions are encouraged, but none more than an hour's drive or less each way, a time that is usually quite long enough on narrow, winding, and high-hedged lanes.

The thumbprint school gives us time to catch our breath, look around a bit, and even settle down, however lightly and briefly, in a bit of England. If a traveler chooses the right base, the English countryside is so full of attractions that a week in one spot is seldom long enough to discover and enjoy them all.

The following section gives several examples of my kind of thumbprint. Note that I describe two different thumbprints in separate parts of Cornwall and again two more in the Highlands. No one can see Cornwall, or indeed any particular section of Great Britain, in just one visit, or one week (or one month, and so on!).

Many counties, or regions of England, vary enormously in the space of an hour's drive, and you may find one county, or part of a *county, that will draw you back again and again. We have been in West Dorset many times (see Chapter Ten, "Dorset Days"), and we still have not seen or done everything we wish we could.*

These thumbprints are meant to suggest how a traveler might spend a week in a particular place. (Sometimes, before you go, you have a hard time imagining what you could do for a whole week in just one spot.) Although we have loved each of these areas, others beckon us too. Another traveler can easily find another rewarding base. Try doing a little pleasant research, choose a village or town or countryside hotel of your own, and you may leave your special thumbprint somewhere on your individual map!

8

A Spyglass on
Padstow Harbor

Readers of My Love Affair with England *may recognize the inscription on the seaside bench. Ida's wistful message haunted me until I decided to dedicate that book, in part, to Henry and Ida.*

ONE DAY, HENRY! LUV, IDA. As I read this cryptic but poignant message engraved on a park bench, the sea wind whipped at my legs. I was high above the harbor of Padstow in North Cornwall, on a town path leading to the coastal cliffs. Villagers often used the wide field below the path for picnics and games; Ida's was only one of several donated benches with plaques.

On this summer evening, stolid and silent figures—villagers, not tourists—were planted on most of the benches. Two women with worn faces and tight-pulled cardigans talked somberly to each other; a frail-looking old man with a cane stared out into the harbor. I thought of Ida's loss, and I wondered if any of them had known Henry. I nodded to the women, who nodded back, and walked on.

That moment in Padstow—a fleeting sense of being part of the ongoing life of a community—was one of the rewards of vacationing for a week in an English village. Our home that mid-June was Padstow, an old fishing port, once one of the busiest towns in Cornwall, on the ancient trade route between Ireland and Europe. Its population eventually declined, but lurched again into sudden growth in recent years. When we first approached Padstow, through its dense and rawly unattractive modern outskirts, James and I looked at each other in alarm. But as soon as we took a steep downward turn toward the cobblestone quay, we knew we were going to enjoy ourselves.

Houses on the Padstow harbor are among the oldest in the community—including a sixteenth-century courthouse where Sir Walter Raleigh once presided—and they huddle together as if for protection from the brazen and threatening world that is rising swiftly around them. We soon were safely ensconced in pink-washed Fo'c'sle Cottage, a stucco storefront building right on the quay.

Fo'c'sle Cottage, recently "done up" for vacationers, had two floors of surprisingly cushy comfort, including dishwasher and VCR, blithely installed among the remaining dark timbered beams. The cottage (really a *holiday flat*) sat above a small traditional tearoom and café. Down-home cooking smells, a mixture of fish and chips and cabbage, occasionally drifted up through our backyard, and a very insistent rock group played just below our bedroom on Saturday night. But we had no doubt we were in the thick of things. The village shops were only moments away, and the fishmonger (not so easy to find in England these days) sold the daily catch at the far end of the pier.

From our front windows we could peek right into the inner harbor, the heart of old Padstow. Our privileged position gave us a private spyglass on everyday life along the quay and in the harbor. Each morning an ancient rusty dredging barge toiled at clearing buckets of sludge from the harbor floor. We listened to the dredgers' shouted banter aboard their dour contraption, which looked about to sink under its own weight. Sometimes a deep sea fishing boat putt-putted past our cottage and deposited a few tourists and assorted fish, including, once, a small bloodied shark. (Shark, however, was *not* on the menu at the fishmonger's that day.)

One afternoon a shouting instructor gave a group of young boys, in what looked like scouting uniforms complete with neckerchiefs, kayak lessons in the harbor. The water churned as they paddled desperately in circles, trying to stay upright. Later a fierce race among girls' rowing clubs began in the tidal estuary and ended below our window. The girls cheered themselves on, splashing and yelling. We watched with sympathy as the last-place crewing shell limped into the harbor. One night a battered wooden sailboat moored outside our door. Where had it come from? An exotic port in the Mediterranean or a marina on the south coast of Cornwall? It disappeared the next morning before we could find out.

On the weekend, British visitors—we saw no Americans—swarmed over the quay with a good-natured holiday air. Families walked back and forth, peering into shopwindows, sampling fudge and ice cream cones, and lining up for speedboat rides around the estuary. On a sunny Sunday afternoon, as we relaxed with after-lunch coffee in Fo'c'sle Cottage, we suddenly heard the rousing sounds of a brass band. It was irresistible. We hurried down our stairs.

At the far end of the quay, a small circle of people gathered around the music makers, who were the town band from nearby Launceston, resplendent in starched white shirts and red or black ties. They had just begun a long and high-spirited concert, attended by passersby, friends, and several proud parents, for some members of the band were quite young.

We admired the determination of a young boy perhaps ten or eleven blowing a trumpet as if his life depended on it, as well as the vigor of a very stout middle-aged woman, concentrated and perspiring, enthusiastically attacking a French horn. They were not really performing for tourists; they were obviously playing with joy mainly for themselves. But we got to listen anyway. Both reminded of Sunday band concerts in our small midwestern towns years ago, James and I applauded appreciatively. Although we'd just eaten, we then decided to treat ourselves, like everyone else on the quay, to ice cream cones.

Besides all the activities in the harbor, we had our choice of many appealing walks right from our cottage door. Wide stretches of sandy beach along the estuary were perfect for strolling and foot-dabbling. One fog-hung morning we slipped down from a path that led from the harbor along the cliffs toward the sea. We padded barefoot in the surprisingly warm, shallow water for almost two hours, curtained by mists and closed off by ourselves in a white, filmy world. The only sound was water slurping quietly over firmly packed sand, as the tide slowly crept higher around our ankles.

The path continued on, high above colorful sailboards and sailboats in the estuary, finally bringing us to a headland with spectacular views up and down the coast. Here we could have joined the dramatic long-distance Cornish coastal path, which circles the peninsula. But such an ambitious jaunt had to wait for another visit. Every evening after dinner, we took a more modest promenade, joining many villagers for an amble up to the War Memorial, a modern granite cross, along a high path lined with benches.

Because it is hard to stay for a week on a harbor and not want to go to sea, we decided one morning to book passage on the *Jubilee Queen*, an excursion boat. Twice daily, weather permitting, it ferries sightseers to Puffin Island, a rocky promontory in turbulent open water just beyond the mouth of the estuary. We did see dozens of whirling orange-beaked birds and nesting sea gulls, although we had to fight for a foothold on the violently tilting deck. (I seemed to be whirling too, and I was glad to return to the calm harbor.)

The estuary at Padstow turns into the Camel River upstream, and after I had recovered from our roller-coaster ride to Puffin Island, I was ready to sail again. One sunny, lazy afternoon, we returned to the *Jubilee Queen*, this time on a river cruise, two sleepy hours to Wadebridge. As we munched a picnic lunch, we watched the gentle hills and woods slip past us and noted a level, nearly deserted footpath that paralleled the river all the way. Next trip, we agreed, we'd walk that path.

Like most English villages, Padstow has its share of local historic sites and houses. Not far from the church, which has a fifteenth-century stone font and an Elizabethan pulpit, is Prideaux Place, a handsome Elizabethan house, complete with deer park, recently opened to the public. Despite its touches of grandeur, the house had a homey and lived-in feeling. Our giggly, friendly guide—we were her only charges— told us, after we'd asked a few questions, a ghost story about the house garnered from someone who knew someone who, working alone late one night, had actually *seen* the silent impression of footsteps slowly descending the stairs and crushing the carpet, step by step.

Exploring outward from Padstow, we discovered pleasures that never appear in guidebooks. A sign in a shop window advertised a COFFEE MORNING AND BAKE SALE in aid of the Royal Lifeboat Association, so one bright morning we drove to St. Merryn, an even smaller nearby village, and joined about twenty local residents in the backyard of an unpretentious house on the main road. There we sipped our coffee, devoured homemade apple tarts and apricot-jam cake, and chatted politely about Minneapolis and Cornwall.

A coffee morning in St. Merryn seems an unlikely occasion for shopping, but this low-key adventure also brought my best bargains of the whole trip. Nosing out the *jumble* (rummage sale) in the upstairs bedrooms, I unearthed a hand-knit mohair sweater (only slightly used) for less than a dollar and a flowery china teacup for fifty cents.

Now definitely in a holiday mood, we drove afterward for fifteen minutes to reach Trevose Head, a magnificent grassy cliff with a lighthouse overlooking a sweep of high green meadow that ends in a crashing sea. A guidebook had informed me that this lighthouse was the last to be run on compressed air and paraffin, but we never got inside. It was too blissful to lie in the clipped green grass near the edge of the cliffs, close our eyes, bask in the sun, and listen to the rough surf smashing against the rocks below.

Following our thumbprint rule, we usually spent part of each day in short trips to country houses and gardens open to the public. In June, before the English school vacation, visitors were few, and we were able to wander the grounds of these great houses as alone and carefree as if we were lords of the manor.

Less than half an hour from Padstow, between Wadebridge

and Bodmin, off the A389 and B3266 at Washaway, Pencarrow, a well-proportioned Georgian house, sits in fifty acres of formal and woodland gardens. To reach it, we drove down a mile-long avenue beneath towering beech trees. Like some other great houses open to the public, Pencarrow is still inhabited by its owners. Although sumptuously furnished from the days of England's great empire, it had a lived-in air.

Unlike the National Trust, Cornwall's major owner of such houses, which allows visitors to wander freely, Pencarrow's management insisted on a guided tour. Such rote tours often make me restless, but this one provided a few engaging details. As we admired the heavy, rich Chinese damask curtains in one room, for example, our lecturer mentioned that they had been made from material purloined by an early owner from a boarded vessel. It was a salutary reminder, linking these grand houses with a buccaneering era when Britain's naval power included profitable acts of piracy. America has no monopoly on robber barons.

When we were standing for a moment beside a back staircase, I was suddenly struck by Pencarrow's elegant airiness. Rising upward in a series of graceful curves, the stairs (leading, I think, to servants' quarters) were bathed in light from carefully placed windows. The back stairs I knew, from a few Victorian houses at home, were cramped, second-rate, and strictly utilitarian. At Pencarrow, the eighteenth-century Palladian architect never skimped.

Outside the house, an enticing path led through a huge woodland garden, a seemingly natural tangle of shrubs and trees. It can be startling to glimpse a clump of tall bamboo on a cold, rainy English day, yet Pencarrow's protected valley shelters not only bamboo but palm trees, rhododendrons (more than six hundred different species), camellias, and a lily-filled little lake. Here at Pencarrow a visitor can also ponder the monkey puzzle tree (*Araucaria araucana*), whose name, my trusty *Good Gardens Guide* informed me, originated here, "when, in 1834, the parliamentary barrister Charles Austin, who was staying at Pencarrow, rashly touched the prickly leaves and quickly withdrew his hand, saying 'It would puzzle a monkey.'"

In contrast to Pencarrow's light-filled elegance, Lanhydrock, Cornwall's self-designated *great house*, is solid, massive and richly Victorian. Now owned by the National Trust, Lanhydrock House stands above the Fowey valley some twenty minutes from Padstow, two and a half miles southeast of Bodmin. A seventeenth-century mansion mostly rebuilt after a fire in 1881, Lanhydrock's forty rooms are furnished as if the Empress of India still triumphantly reigned.

I was awed by the master bath with its enormous mahogany-framed tub, so big it needed a set of steps to its rim. His lady's magnificent maple dressing table was laid with a sterling-silver set of brushes, combs, cosmetic pots, and mirrors that would have required more than one lady's maid, I thought, to sort out and wield efficiently. At the other end of the social scale, I saw that the spare servants' rooms on an upper floor were much smaller than the nearby spacious attic compartment set aside for the lord's collection of massive luggage.

Coming from such darkly ponderous luxury, I was startled to enter the seventeenth-century Long Gallery. Untouched by the fire, this 116-foot room was decorated with a ceiling of embossed plaster reliefs that detailed Old Testament stories amid fantastical birds and beasts. The Renaissance plasterwork was so lavishly high-spirited that I put a near-permanent crick in my neck peering up to see it. Afterward, we recovered by ambling among roses and sculptured yews in the thirty-acre garden.

Because distances in England are often surprisingly small, we could sometimes visit more than one house or garden in a single afternoon. Leaving Padstow after lunch one day, we combined a stop at one of Cornwall's most famous gardens, Trewithen, and, not far away, an Elizabethan manor house, Trerice.

Trewithen, on Grampound Road near Truro, just off the A390, another Cornish spot so favored in climate that it shelters exotic trees and shrubs, has a secluded atmosphere. This is a garden meant to be enjoyed by the family who created it, not so much a showpiece as a personal retreat, filled with flowering shrubs and rare trees. (*The Good Gardens Guide* rattled off a one-line inventory that sounded like an indecipherable incantation: "There are many nothofagus, embothriums, pieris, enkianthus, eucryphias, griselinias." I'm sure there were.)

Trewithen's founder, George Johnstone, affectionately named some plants after members of his family and staff—"Alison Johnstone" rhododendron, for example. I briefly pondered what it might be like to hear someone pausing at one of the daylilies in my own garden at home and saying, "This light red one with fading yellow streaks is Susan Toth."

Trewithen's luxurious tranquillity is enhanced by spacious lawns, a surrounding open park, and wooded long views in every direction. Although I haven't ridden a horse in years, I began to picture myself cantering lightly through the park, then returning before supper for a leisurely walk among the rare rhododendrons, greeting each by name. ("Good evening,

Alison; hello, Elizabeth; have you had a pleasant day, Jack Skelton?")

Like Trewithen, Trerice, about three miles southeast of Newquay, also seems shielded from heavy traffic and streams of visitors. We approached the house via a narrow, twisting, high-banked lane, as if our destination were in an enchanted enclosure.

Trerice was neither as grand as Lanhydrock nor as studiously graceful as Pencarrow, but it had a domestic charm, from its trellised pink roses on the warm gray exterior stone to a small walled garden. Several centuries ago, Trerice's gardeners had planted an orchard, in a Renaissance quincunx pattern (four trees each forming the corner of a square, one tree in the middle). It is still maintained, with apples, pears, quince, and plums. Trerice's garden was the kind of place where we could sit on a garden bench and comfortably eat our sandwiches.

Like Lanhydrock, Trerice boasted an elaborate plastered ceiling ("as fine as any in the West Country," the brochure said proudly) in its hall as well as a great east window with almost six hundred leaded panes, much of it original glass. Also like Lanhydrock, Trerice is owned by the National Trust, so we could roam on our own through its rooms, trying to imagine what it might be like to sit and read below the leaded-glass windows.

Behind the house, an ancient stone barn of majestic proportions had been converted into a simple but pleasant restaurant. Next to it, housed in a former stable, was a modest museum that seemed quirkily English, with an annotated collection of lawn mowers of different sizes and periods. Walking with some bemusement among various clipping and slicing devices, wooden rollers, and early gasoline engines, we managed to absorb a surprising amount of countryside history.

By six o'clock that evening, after returning from Trewithen and Trerice, the crowded day melted away into the peace of our Padstow cottage. As we sat in our tiny timbered dining room, listening to the gentle murmur of villagers' voices on the quay outside, we tucked gratefully into our fresh hake, English beets, Cornish new potatoes, wholegrain buns from our friendly baker, and a dessert of small, juicy local strawberries. It was the kind of meal we find only when we cook for ourselves in our own—if temporary—home.

After dinner we walked slowly in the dusk up the seaward path. I paused at Ida's bench, now a familiar landmark. "One day, Ida!" I promised, giving quiet thanks for our week in Padstow. I told her we'd be back.

A FEW FLOATING FACTS

A note on distances: Rather than make a seven- or eight-hour drive (or longer, depending on weather and chance) from a London airport to Cornwall, we always prefer to stop overnight somewhere in Devon or Dorset. The M roads go only so far, and, once off them, traffic can be very slow.

For information on how to rent a holiday flat like Fo'c'sle Cottage, see Chapter One, "How to Be Your Own Travel Agent."

9

Hidden Corners in Du Maurier Country

When I first read Daphne Du Maurier, I knew I would someday have to go to Cornwall. In *Jamaica Inn*, *Frenchman's Creek*, and, above all, *Rebecca*, Du Maurier beckoned me into a land of moonlit moors and dangerously stormy seas, of dark, forbidding forests, of ancient footpaths and twisting roads, of ivy-covered cottages and haunted stone mansions. I was perhaps twenty, a perfect age to discover Du Maurier. Although she disliked the adjective *romantic*—she specifically rejected it for two nonfiction titles, in favor of *Vanishing Cornwall* and *Enchanted Cornwall*—Du Maurier's Cornwall is mysterious and magical.

When after many years I arrived in Du Maurier country, I found to my delight that much of her Cornwall is still there. Some of it has indeed vanished, as she feared, for both British and foreign tourists flock to its picturesque seaside villages every summer, and the relentless pressure of too many visitors has left its mark, in holiday cottages, trailer parks, crowded parking areas, and entertainment facilities. The widely advertised Great Cornish Holiday Trail includes such inventions as the Flambards Village Theme Park, St. Agnes Leisure Park,

DairyLand Farm World, Automobilia, and World of Model Railways.

But in late spring or early summer, before British schools are out, certain corners of Cornwall can be blissfully quiet. It is a perfect time to follow the footsteps of Du Maurier down country lanes, across flowering fields, and along the rocky, spectacular coast.

One April James and I rented a National Trust holiday cottage for a week on the coast near Helston, not far from Penzance. I had not planned our trip with any conscious memories of Du Maurier. But as we were driving toward Helston, I studied my detailed map. "We're staying not far from Helford," I said thoughtfully to James. "I think that's where Mary Yellan in *Jamaica Inn* came from." A brooding, bitter tale about a courageous young woman who unwillingly becomes involved with a gang of smugglers, *Jamaica Inn* (1936) was Du Maurier's first novel set in Cornwall.

Mary had loved Helford, a small village on a sheltered stretch of river. Forced to live with her aunt on rougher, wilder Bodmin Moor, deep in the interior of Cornwall, Mary recalled her old home with longing, with its green hills and sloping valleys, and a "white cluster of cottages at the water's edge."

A few days later, James was nosing the car slowly down an excruciatingly narrow lane toward Helford. This was indeed the gentle face of Cornwall, with scattered small villages, steeply sloping farms, and densely latticed woodland along the Helford River, a quiet estuary. On an early sunny April morning, with dew still dripping from the overhanging trees, the countryside seemed remote, untouched, and tranquil, much as

Du Maurier must have first seen it when she settled in Cornwall as a young woman in the late 1920s.

Leaving the car outside the village, whose ribbon-thin lanes are closed to outside traffic, we walked past Helford's "white cluster of cottages"—the picturesque houses still huddle together at the river's edge—and headed for a footpath that led to the sea. For two hours we circled the headlands that overlook the estuary and coast.

Although the day was sunny and breezy, long spring rains had thoroughly soaked the ground. Tramping along our narrow path, which was sometimes a barely visible beaten line through tall grass, and often a dark tunnel between high hedges and overshadowing trees, we frequently sank into inches of mud. Occasionally all signs of the path were swallowed up in mire, and I clutched my Ordnance Survey Pathfinder map as if we might never find our way home again.

But we did not dream of turning back. Wildflowers bloomed in hedgerows and in the fields we crossed, and seemingly endless bluebells in the woods glinted in shafts of sunlight that sparkled through the trees. Sometimes the ground shimmered as if bright bits of blue sky had fallen into the intensely green grass. In *Rebecca* (1938), Du Maurier's famous novel of jealousy and deception, Maxim takes his new bride to Manderley in late spring, "arriving with the first swallows and the bluebells." He knew she would see Cornwall then at its most beguiling.

When we emerged onto the headlands, a light wind whipped up waves that broke against the rocky cliffs. The water was a constantly changing tint, turquoise to dark green to blue again, first glimmering in the sun and then darkening when clouds passed overhead. We could see two or three white sails floating in the far distance, as well as a bulky freighter slowly moving across the horizon. Decades ago, one of those sails might have been Du Maurier's, for she and her husband loved to explore the coastline in their twenty-foot cruiser, *Ygdrasil*, or their sailing ketch, *Restless*.

Our path sometimes dipped down to tiny coves, where the sea rolled across a pebbly shore. The air was fresh and almost warm, and the sea seemed deceptively friendly as it lapped softly at our feet. No wonder Mary Yellan was homesick on Bodmin Moor, which seemed to her in contrast "a scrubby land, without hedgerow or meadow; a country of stones, black heather, and stunted broom."

James and I had driven through Bodmin Moor several years before on our way to Padstow. Bodmin lies between the coasts in the heart of Cornwall. Like Dartmoor and Exmoor, Bodmin has its own eerie beauty, with untamed expanses of boggy and bracken-strewn wasteland and towering outcroppings of eroded rock.

On that earlier trip we had stopped at Jamaica Inn, a striking sight as it rises from the wild open moor all around it. Unfortunately, the old rambling stone inn is now a tourist mecca, with restaurants like Smuggler's Bar and Pedlar's Snack Bar, a gift shop, and a Victorian Museum of Curiosity that includes a two-headed lamb. Its parking area is filled with crowded buses rather than smugglers' wagons. Jamaica Inn had failed to renew my interest in Du Maurier.

But as James and I walked the coast near Helford that morning in April, I felt almost as if Du Maurier were whispering some kind of reminder to me. I thought of her fierce love of the sea, and of my own. She was one of several writers who, like Sarah Orne Jewett, Joseph Conrad, and Virginia Woolf, had stirred in my landlocked midwestern imagination a longing to live by an ocean—or at least escape there as often as possible.

The changing moods of the sea are almost always part of Du Maurier's landscape, and her novels are filled with a sense of impending fate that seems reinforced by the constant rhythm of the tides. In *Frenchman's Creek* (1941), for instance, a story about a dashing French pirate and a high-spirited aristocrat who falls in love with him, the pirate Aubéry's successful forays all depend on his catching the rising tide, which allows his ship to sail down the creek to the sea. Even on Bodmin Moor the sea is not far away, as Mary Yellan sees in *Jamaica Inn*, when once, after climbing a high tor, she looks beyond the rolling moors, which seem like an immense desert, to a faint silver light on the horizon.

The sea in Du Maurier country is not always peaceful. In *Jamaica Inn* the storm-tossed Cornish coast turns savage, as wreckers, cold-blooded and desperate men, set false lights to lure ships to their destruction. Even in *Rebecca*, where the sea plays a less important role, a shipwreck in a smothering fog brings about the dramatic climax of the story, when Rebecca's body is found.

Our week's home in Du Maurier country almost seemed part of the encroaching sea. Bar Lodge, a handsome Victorian stone house, stood high on a lonely hill overlooking a wide stretch of sand called the Loe Bar. No one lived near us. A public footpath passed in front of the house, leading to the small fishing village of Porthleven, half a mile away, or, in the other direction, along the unspoiled, hilly coastline toward Gunwalloe. Traffic was nonexistent; only a rough, rocky track led from a discreet gate at the entrance of the National Trust's Penrose Estate to a dead end at our front door.

From our rooftop terrace we saw nothing but the sea—no houses, no farms, not even grazing sheep. The sea dissolved into an infinite horizon. Constant waves crashed upon the sandbar below, which formed a barrier that long ago had created an unusual body of water. Loe Pool, once an estuary, widened behind the narrow bar into Cornwall's largest freshwater lake, a refuge for wildfowl—ducks, mute swans, cormorants, herons, and others. The Loe was silent, but the ocean was not. At night, as we lay in bed in the stunningly deep darkness, we fell asleep to the sound of the sea.

Although I had not intended to make our week at Bar Lodge a literary pilgrimage, after our excursion to Mary Yellan's Helford, I felt I could no more ignore Du Maurier than the insistent clamor of the sea. After combing a bookshop in Penzance for copies of Du Maurier's Cornish novels, I began rereading.

Du Maurier captured me once more with her uncanny storytelling, a narrative momentum that hurtles over occasionally bumpy plots, melodramatic incidents, and enigmatic characters. I sensed, too, the powerful though unarticulated melancholy that runs throughout her stories like an underground river. An indistinguishable part of her Cornish landscapes, it carries a sense of the uncertainty of happiness and the almost unbearable transitoriness of time.

As James and I continued to delve deeper into her Cornwall, Du Maurier's haunting stories stayed with us. One day we explored Frenchman's Creek, a narrow inlet not far from Helford, overhung by tangled shrubs and thick woods. A path runs beside the creek, following its turnings until it emerges

into the full light of the Helford estuary. We found it as lovely
as did Dona, the heroine of *Frenchman's Creek*, for whom the
creek was a thrilling surprise, "still and soundless, shrouded
by the trees, hidden from the eyes of men."

Since most of *Frenchman's Creek* takes place near Helford,
some miles away from Bar Lodge, I was startled to find that
the final scene of the novel unfolds at Loe Pool. (Du Maurier
calls it the Looe, perhaps because her home in Cornwall was
close to Looe Bay and its twin ports of East Looe and West
Looe.) From our terrace I could easily imagine where the pirate Aubéry and Dona parted for the last time. Although a
few visitors sometimes came to the beach—only a few, since a
sign warned of fierce undercurrents and forbade swimming—
they always left by dusk. At night, when we stood on the terrace
to watch the fading sheen of sky and water, the shore looked as
untouched and remote as it might have on that imagined night
in the late seventeenth century, when Dona and her pirate slept
by their campfire. To Du Maurier, the Loe was a symbol of the
hidden, mysterious Cornwall that always awaits the right visitor, sometimes just beyond the next turning.

One day James and I took the morning to hike around the
Loe's five-mile perimeter. The footpath led through varied
landscape, from pastureland to dark woods to a reedy shoreline along a wide marsh. Once at the far end of the lake, we
could no longer see the ocean, and as we crossed the marsh on
a causeway, the landscape turned unfamiliar. A National
Trust brochure about the Loe accurately remarks: "The tangle of water-tolerant trees—willow and alder—is reminiscent
of a tropical mangrove swamp, and one would not be a bit surprised to see the snout of a crocodile protruding from the
murky shallows."

The last part of the path around the Loe reminded me of *Rebecca*. As the path turned into our private road, it wound tortuously for a mile along the banks of the lake, under a shadowy canopy of tall pines. A similar approach to Manderley made the unnamed narrator think of a path in the forest in a Grimms' fairy tale, where "it's always longer than one expects, and the trees are so dark, and close."

Mysterious Manderley is one of the most famous houses in English literature. Few readers of *Rebecca* forget its hypnotic opening: "Last night I dreamt I went to Manderley again." Du Maurier's main inspiration for Manderley was Menabilly, an old house with Tudor origins set in secluded woods back from the sea on the Gribbin peninsula, near Fowey. It was Du Maurier's home for twenty-five years.

Menabilly is not open to the public, although I wish I could have wandered its grounds and peeked through its windows as Du Maurier did, years before she leased it as a near ruin. But we did glimpse other grand houses and gardens, some of whose sites and extensive grounds gave us hints of what Menabilly/Manderley might have been like. Under the National Gardens Scheme, several houses near the Loe held open days in their gardens during the week of our stay. At Polgwynne, near Feock, we took a leisurely stroll around the formal lawns edged with brilliantly flowering shrubs. From the lawns the house looked down upon Carrick Roads, a wide inlet of the sea, gleaming that day with white sails. Polgwynne had a stately air that might have been Manderley's.

At Carclew Gardens, between Falmouth and Truro, we slipped briefly into the past, as often happens in Cornwall. On a barred side road near the entrance to the garden, we saw from a distance the derelict shell of the old manor house, which, like Manderley, had long ago burned down. Now, covered with ivy, the ruin stood among weeds and untended trees, its imposing columns and gaping windows an arresting façade in a domestic green jungle.

Another afternoon, at Trebah Garden, one of Cornwall's showpieces, we had a glimpse of what Manderley's surrounding parkland might have been like. Trebah, outside Mawnan Smith, near Falmouth, drifts across twenty-five acres of ravine, with changing views over hydrangeas, azaleas, and rhododendrons, down to a rain forest of giant tree ferns, bananas, and bamboo. Past pools with flashing orange-gold carp, its paths descend the steep ravine, merging and turning through bowers of flowering shrubs until they end at a sheltered beach on the Helford River. There, with the estuary of the sea before us, we could look back up the ravine over masses of scarlet, pink, and white blossoms.

At Trebah, I felt we had found Manderley's Happy Valley. This is an idyllic wooded retreat where Maxim takes his new wife, and it, too, leads to the sea. The narrator remembers brushing the dripping heads of azaleas as she passes along the path, and when she emerges into a little cove, with hard white shingle underfoot and water breaking on the shore, she is surprised and dazzled. She could have been standing at the foot of Trebah.

Not every excursion during our week at Bar Lodge led directly into a Du Maurier novel. Other explorations were more lighthearted (as indeed she herself could be). She might have been both touched and pleased by the Seal Sanctuary at Gweek, a rescue center for gray Atlantic seals, as well as a home for sea lions, penguins, abandoned donkeys, and a sheep called Monty. The sanctuary provides medical treatment and convalescent pens for its rescued animals, almost all of which are eventually weaned and released to the wild. Located in a green and peaceful setting on the upper reaches of the Helford River, its interpretive center and cheerful outdoor pools are open to visitors.

Since Du Maurier loved to walk by the sea, she also would have approved of our many rambles that week in our little part of Cornwall. According to her biographer, Margaret Forster, Du Maurier cherished her routines, which she called her *routes*, and we, too, came to depend on our daily hike from Bar Lodge along the side of the seaside cliffs into the village of Porthleven, where we could pick up a newspaper, fresh crab, another head of lettuce, or a bottle of wine.

On our last day we took a longer walk, one that was a final reminder of the mysterious magic of Du Maurier country. Although Lizard Point, at the tip of a peninsula that is the most southerly point of Britain, is supposed to be a mecca for tourists in midsummer, in April it was almost deserted. Beginning just below the Lizard's lighthouse, which guards some of the most treacherous rocks along the coast, we hiked along the coastal path to Kynance Cove.

The path dipped up and down at the edge of the sea, sometimes high above inaccessible sandy coves, sometimes across jagged rock formations. Other rocky islets hovered in the fog just off shore. Despite the warmth of the morning, with bright sunshine that frequently burned through, the mists were thick enough so that the lighthouse, now vanished from sight, kept sounding a wild warning blast. We could not see very far, and the path ahead dissolved in the mist.

Wildflowers were sparkling everywhere in the thick, tough carpet of grass that led almost to the precipitous slope of the rocky cliffs. As we walked along the path, the sun often on our backs and the sound of the sea always below us, I felt, very sat-isfyingly, as if we were at the end of the world.

Before turning toward home, we sat on a rocky ledge just below the booming foghorn of the lighthouse, eating our packed lunch and jumping a little at each blast. I was tired but happy. As I munched my tuna fish sandwich and drank in the damp ocean air, I was glad to remember that the rocks and sea had been here long before Du Maurier had walked in Corn-wall. They would be here long after we had gone.

Even in our brief week, we, too, had come to know some-thing of the spirit of Du Maurier's Cornwall. In 1989, at the end of her life, Du Maurier wrote: "I walked this land with a dreamer's freedom and with a waking man's perception—places, houses whispered to me their secrets and shared with me their sorrows and their joys. And in return I gave them something of myself, a few of my novels passing into the folk-lore of this ancient place." We were grateful we had been able to share, for a very short time, her dreamer's freedom in the land she had so loved.

A FEW FLOATING FACTS

For information on how to rent a cottage such as Bar Lodge from the National Trust, see Chapter One, "How to Be Your Own Travel Agent."

Margaret Forster's authorized biography, *Daphne Du Mau-rier*, published in 1993, describes Du Maurier's turbulent life (1907–1989), her years in Cornwall, and her books. Du Mau-rier herself wrote two books about Cornwall: *Vanishing Corn-wall* (1967, reissued 1981) and *Enchanted Cornwall* (1989).

10

Dorset Days

"Y ou're going to spend a week in England *where?*" an incredulous friend asked.

"A tiny village called Chedington," I said again.

My friend shook her head. "Never heard of it. What in the world will you find to *do* there?"

I smiled.

Tucked into the deep hills of western Dorset, just off the major tourist routes across England, Chedington is so small that its handful of cottages doesn't even appear on some large-scale maps. Here, far from the crowds that haunt Blenheim Palace, Stonehenge, Stratford-upon-Avon, or Haworth, I find the England of my dreams—quiet, pastoral, and sometimes endearingly eccentric.

The first surprise about Chedington is Chedington Court, a country-house hotel itself so deliberately obscure that on our first visit we got lost trying to find it. Even when we stumbled onto the village, we almost missed the hotel's unobtrusive sign. Entering the grounds is like sinking into a reverie of the past, the leisurely world of nineteenth-century country-house weekends. To the right is a long grassy terrace where ladies in sweeping gowns might have walked in the moonlight. At the front of the house, sitting on another terrace, we sip tea while savoring miles of view over the fields and meadows of three counties.

Chedington Court's ten-acre garden, complete with summerhouse, duck pond, stream, flowers, and giant ancient yew hedges, offers its own small surprise, a peculiar memento mori. The grounds were once the local churchyard, and a few decayed tombstones covered with lichen still rise, with a Victorian air of solemn remonstrance, among the carefully tended shrubs and lawn.

Hiding away in Chedington Court, with its ten luxurious bedrooms, large library, sitting room, and conservatory, is so pleasant that I occasionally long for a rainy day so we will have an excuse to stay indoors, perhaps in the library next to a roaring fire. But we are always tempted away. Within a half hour's drive of Chedington are historic towns, majestic country houses, enchanting but almost unvisited gardens, historic sites, and idyllic walking paths.

Beaminster, for example, a small market town just ten minutes away, was Thomas Hardy's Emminster in *Tess of the D'Urbervilles*. Beaminster's stone-roofed market cross, decorated and pinnacled sixteenth-century church tower, and leafy river walks preserve the town's ancient charm.

One path in Beaminster leads along the back of town to Parnham House, regularly open to the public. This elaborate Tudor mansion has become the very modern home, workshop, and residential school of John Makepeace, a famous designer of contemporary furniture, who cuts, shapes, and polishes pieces not only from common woods like oak, ash, and cherry, but also from holly, yew, ripple sycamore, and laburnum.

A tour of the house, past Makepeace's polished desks, tables, and chairs (tagged with prices that could make Tudor antiques seem reasonable), culminated for me at an unexpected sight: an antique dentist's chair in Makepeace's private bathroom. Wary enough so that I bring self-hypnotic tapes to every teeth-cleaning, I could not imagine stumbling at night from bad dreams into a bathroom dominated by a dentist's chair. Ah, I thought bemusedly, English eccentricity lives.

From the master bedroom, almost filled by a huge Makepeace bed made from a single English yew and hung with soft beige wool curtains, I looked out the window to the front garden. An imposing arrangement of clipped yews stood like sentinels on the lawns, with narrow channels of water slipping down the garden between them. This formal terrace gave way to other, smaller gardens, a lake and wilder woodland. I wondered if it would be possible for anyone to remain humble if he or she awoke in the morning in such a bed and to such a view.

A mere three miles from Parnham, but so removed in feeling and atmosphere that it might be in a different world, is another Tudor country house called Mapperton. But while Parnham has resolutely entered the modern world, Mapperton remains in a dream of silence. To find the house, one must consult a very detailed map, watch for almost-undetectable signposts, and follow several hedged lanes nearly too narrow for just one car. These roads give no hint of leading anywhere in particular, until suddenly a tree-lined drive opens toward Mapperton.

We go to Mapperton for its garden. Almost unknown, Mapperton is not the largest, grandest, or most diverse garden near Chedington, but it has the most captivating atmosphere. Before descending steep stone stairs to the first terrace, I always pause to look down the unexpected vista. A formal Italianate sunken garden first created in the 1920s, it gradually grows less formal and wilder as it moves down the valley, until it finally blends into the quiet surrounding hills. Set so intimately in a rolling pastoral landscape, the carved yews, rectangular beds, and statuary are startling in their artifice.

No one ever seems to be around; in a half-dozen visits to Mapperton, we have encountered only three or four people. Soon after it was created in 1920, flappers and their handsome young men must have strolled through this new garden, laughing and talking, sipping drinks in the shade of the cave-like niches in the walls. Now only silent stone creatures—lions, eagles, cranes, mythical gryphons, all pitted and marred by seventy years of weather—keep a lonely watch over moss-edged ponds and faded brick walls.

Nearby are other grand houses and gardens, each with its own appeal. Forde Abbey, near Chard, once a Cistercian monastery, was converted into a country house in the mid-seventeenth century. It still has a curiously monastic air, enhanced by its old walls of mellowed rosy brick, but the vast gardens (more than thirty acres) have a luxurious ease. Paths lead to a bog garden thick with primulas (primrose) and many exotic Asian plants, a rock garden, and an ornamental lake. Swans glide gracefully on a pond whose banks are dotted in spring by thousands of crocuses and daffodils.

At Barrington Court, a Tudor manor house near Ilminster, the National Trust leases the interior space to an upscale firm specializing in antique furniture reproductions. Since we quickly tired of looking at expensive fakes, we instead spent most of our time very happily in the gardens, a series of "rooms" in the style of Gertrude Jekyll. For walkers, a path wanders over the estate, which spreads over two hundred acres.

Brympton d'Evercy, tucked away in the countryside near Yeovil, fully lives up to its aristocratic name, with a gracious house, part Tudor, part seventeenth century, in a tranquil setting. An English critic once said of it: "I know no other house of which the whole impression is more lovely and none that summarises so exquisitely English country life." (It is currently open by appointment only.) Its south front, with a long double row of magnificent windows, opens onto a lawn and terraces that calmly sweep to a reflecting pond edged by iris and jeweled with waterlilies.

Although the house at Clapton Court, near Crewkerne, is not open to the public, its garden is a treasure. A winding path loops through a wooded glade, climbing a small slope that reveals in turn azaleas, rhododendron, primroses, iris, geraniums, and many rarer plants. A small stream is diverted into a series of brooks whose liquid sound is always in the background. Because the garden has so many unexpected turnings, flowering nooks with benches, and changing vistas, it seems much more extensive than it really is. The tour of the garden ends with a view of the oldest and largest ash tree in England.

To visit Montacute House, four miles west of Yeovil, is to reenter the Tudor past. Its twisted Tudor chimneypots tower over a series of formal gardens with clipped yews and green lawns, edged by pasture and parkland. After admiring the Renaissance plasterwork, heraldic glass, and carved paneling of the house, we ascended to a series of rooms where the National Portrait Gallery has lent most of its collection of Elizabethan and Jacobean portraits. Suddenly the house came alive.

Here were Cecil, Raleigh, More, Henry VIII, Elizabeth, Essex—the great names, and faces, of that turbulent and fabled time. As I studied these canny statesmen, powerful bish-

ops, bejeweled courtiers, and of course the Virgin Queen herself, I could easily see them pacing through these paneled
rooms, gossiping in pairs in front of the hanging tapestries,
or dancing gracefully down the upper gallery. The gallery,
dizzyingly long, with windows overlooking the front lawns, is
so light and spacious that even on a busy summer Sunday,
tourists walking through it seem to disappear.

On the way home from Montacute to Chedington, we always
stop at East Lambrook Manor in South Petherton, which offers
an enlightening contrast to Montacute's grandeur. The late
Marjorie Fish, who created the garden around this medieval
manor, is considered the dean of twentieth-century cottage gar-
dening. East Lambrook is a crazy quilt of informally massed
colors, bound with brilliant green lawn. Yet the garden has obviously been planned with an artist's eye for height, shape, shading, and texture. In a space not much bigger than some large
suburban lots, almost every inch has been turned into garden,
with blooms seeming to tumble over each other.

What is so remarkable about Mrs. Fish's garden is how se-
questered it feels. The narrow paths are cleverly laid out,
banked here by tall clipped yews, there by shrubs or hedges or
low walls, angling here along a tiny streambed, there through
an orchard. As soon as we turn a corner, we wander into another sheltered section. It is easy to have the seductive sensation
of suddenly escaping into a secret world of lavender, geraniums, and primulas, where no one could find us for hours.

Arriving at Minterne, a parklike garden not far from Dorchester at Minterne Magna, is part of its pleasure. From Chedington, we edge along back roads through peaceful Dorset
countryside, into deep valleys with picturesque villages like
Evershot, Holywell, and Cerne Abbas (the latter famous for a

giant chalk figure on its hillside). Minterne itself is best in the spring, when its mile-and-a-half path leads through flowering azaleas and rhododendrons, then along a musical stream thickly shaded by water-loving plants.

When I am searching out the treasures of western Dorset, I always find myself eventually at the sea. Southeast of Chedington, the Abbotsbury Gardens, near Weymouth, with twenty acres in a sheltered seaside location, is famous for rare subtropical plants, peacocks, and attractive walks. (Since it is well known, you may find a bus tour or two.)

Nearby is the Abbotsbury Swannery, where monks once raised a colony of mute swans. The family who has owned the swannery since 1541 still nurtures and protects them. From a carefully sited path through the swannery, visitors can see, at different times, nests, young goslings, and proud adult birds serenely sailing on the water.

Dorset offers many ways to walk along the sea. Although Lyme Regis, with its literary associations (Jane Austen loved Lyme, and John Fowles set *The French Lieutenant's Woman* there), is lively and picturesque, it is hardly unvisited. We prefer Seatown, a hamlet bisected by the busy A35. The whizzing traffic gives no hint that a quick turnoff to the left—almost unmarked and easily missed—will lead through crooked back streets and over several hills to one of the most glorious coastlines in England.

Unlike bustling Lyme Regis, Seatown's sea front has only a parking lot and one pub—no boardwalk, pier, or amusement parlors. What unobtrusive Seatown offers is immediate access to the Dorset Coastal Path, a wonderful walker's trail that edges the ocean along the high limestone cliffs that make this section of coastline so dramatic. Starting from the parking lot, a casual walker, supplied only with comfortable shoes and a windproof jacket, can hike up the cliffs in less than an hour to the top of the Golden Cap, the highest point along the entire south coast. From the windblown Golden Cap, the shore of England disappears into an infinite horizon.

Below on the beach, after clambering over shifting, slippery pebbles, a lowland walker will eventually reach a series of stony ledges, mostly uncovered only at low tide, where fossil hunters often tap away at the gray-blue crumbling rock. Standing on one of these ledges, listening to the rush of the ocean and looking down at the clear imprints of long-extinct marine life, I had a fleeting sense of time and space extending far beyond my comprehension.

Another walk that leads to a place with intimations of silence and strangeness, Pilsdon Pen, is only fifteen minutes from Chedington. There an Iron Age earthwork fort was once established on the top of a hill that is the highest point of inland Dorset. A short, steep path ascends Pilsdon Pen, where, on a clear day, the view flows over lush green hills and valleys all the way to the English Channel and, to the west, Dartmoor. We scaled Pilsdon Pen in a soft rain, and I could easily imagine that the fog-shrouded hill was somehow haunted by the long-ago people who huddled here for security. We were not surprised to learn later that a local white witch sometimes conducts services on the top of the hill.

Fortunately, since western Dorset gets its share of English rain, not every attraction is outdoors. One soggy afternoon, we drove half an hour to Compton House, the home of Worldwide Butterflies and Lullingstone Silk Farm. I have always loved silk, and I was curious to see how it was made. Few tourists were here, and no Americans: just lots of worms and butterflies. Behind glass cases, we watched silkworms hatching, feasting, and spinning their silk, which is then harvested and wound on large spools. With typical British thoroughness, the process is illustrated with educational placards. (One placard notes with pride that Lullingstone's well-fed worms supplied the silk for Princess Diana's wedding gown.)

But Lullingstone, too, had its unexpected moment. In another set of rooms, butterflies and moths live out their short life cycle. A young woman serving as commentator and guide showed us a large colorful butterfly clinging to her sweater. It was a weird sight, a live butterfly serving as a temporary ornament. We looked at it closely, admiring its brilliantly patterned wings. It had just hatched that day, she said, and would live only twenty-four hours. By tomorrow at this time, it would be gone.

Rather thoughtful, we decided to end our afternoon in Sherborne Abbey, in the heart of a town some call the most beautiful in Dorset, because it has so many medieval buildings of golden Hamstone. The abbey is noted for its fifteenth-century stone fan-vaulted roof, which soars overhead in the English Gothic tradition. Unlike the great cathedrals of Salisbury and Canterbury, Sherborne doesn't attract hordes of tourists. On the afternoon of our visit, a choirmaster was rehearsing young boys in choral anthems. As we sat almost alone in the dim light filtering through stained-glass windows and listened to their high voices soar upward to the overarching roof, we knew that we were in a church.

Each time we come to Chedington, we try to visit new places as well as old favorites. We never have time for everything: Penelope Hobhouse's Tintinhull Garden; the oddly endearing zoo at Cricket St. Thomas Wildlife Park; the faded gentility of Sidmouth, a seaside resort complete with promenade and bathers; Cadhay Manor at Ottery St. Mary; Sherborne Castle; Hardy's Cottage; Milton Abbey; the rope-making museum at Bridport—my list always grows longer.

So when my friend asked me "What will you *do* for a whole week in a little place like Chedington?" I didn't know how to answer. I could have taken most of our lunchtime to describe the possibilities, and then I would have had to remember and acknowledge, regretfully, that we couldn't do it all. A week under this Dorset thumbprint is never enough.

A FEW FLOATING FACTS

Remember to omit the prefix "0" from an English telephone number when calling from the United States. Prices are calculated at $1.60 to the pound.

To locate many of these houses and gardens, I use an annual directory, *Historic Houses, Castles & Gardens*, published by Reed Information Services (Windsor Court, East Grinstead House, East Grinstead, West Sussex RH19 1XA fax 03142-335720). Widely available in American bookstores with travel sections, it is also sold at many bookstores in England. This large handbook lists over 1300 historic properties in Great Britain and Ireland and gives open times, admission charges, and maps. In 1995 it cost £8.20 (about $13).

Where to Stay in and Around Chedington

Chedington Court, a country-house hotel, offers half board (gourmet dinner, bed, and breakfast) for about £82 ($131) per person per night, with reductions for longer stays. A member of Romantik Hotels. Write or call Mr. or Mrs. Philip Chapman, Chedington Court, Beaminster, Dorset DT8 3HY, telephone Corscombe 01935-891265, fax Corscombe 01935-891442.

An excellent pub lunch within a short walk of Chedington can be found at **Winyard's Gap Inn**, where a plate of Bridport smoked mackerel or savoury mince and mushroom pie with potatoes and fresh vegetables will cost about $8.

In nearby Beaminster, the **Bridge House Hotel**, scheduled as an ancient monument, probably dates from the thirteenth century. The extensively modernized hotel has three categories of rooms, small, standard, and deluxe, with bed and breakfast per person from £56 ($89.60) to £92 ($147.20). Reductions for longer stays. The Bridge House Hotel, Beaminster, Dorset DT8 3AY, telephone 01308-862200.

The Manor House, hidden behind a high wall in the heart of Beaminster, extends to a beautiful garden with lake and waterfalls. Eve and Angus Nicoll grow all their vegetables without chemicals or fertilizers. Bed and breakfast from £26 ($41.60) per person; a half-tester bed with private bathroom slightly higher. Mr. and Mrs. J. A. Nicoll, The Manor House, Beaminster, Dorset DT8 3DZ, telephone 01308-862311.

Jenny Wren's in Beaminster offers bed and breakfast from £16.50 ($26.40) per person, with three bedrooms, including two with private bath. It is located in one of the town's main streets: 1 Hogshill Street, Beaminster, Dorset DT8 AE, telephone 01308-862814. A tiny village next to Chedington, South Perrott, offers B&B at **Hunter's Hatch,** with four rooms, including one with private bath, at £15 ($24) per person. Write or call Mrs. Sandra Horswell at 01935-891352.

Yes, I Know Scotland Is Not England: An Explanatory Note

Scotland is not really part of England, although it formed a legal alliance with Great Britain—England, Scotland, Wales, and Northern Ireland—through the Act of Union in 1707. These comprise the United Kingdom or "U.K." Scotland's remoteness, scattered population, and vast stretches of uninhabited land often make it seem a foreign country, quite different from the thickly settled, often industrial, and more compact English territory south of the border.

And for centuries Scotland was a foreign country, as anyone who reads Scottish history soon discovers. A true Scot would not take kindly to any traveler (or writer) who unthinkingly assumed that England and Scotland were geographically, historically, or culturally unified.

But I have decided to include the following two essays on Scotland in this independent guide for travelers because so many American visitors to England do not make this distinction. Especially to many first-time travelers, England and Great Britain seem synonymous. In planning a trip to England, they often auto-

matically want to add Edinburgh, Glasgow, and sometimes the Lowlands or Border country to their itineraries.

The region of Scotland that has always fascinated me is the lesser-known Highlands, and I would like to encourage others to venture north to explore its unspoiled beauty. My first suggested "thumbprint" covers the area around Gairloch, on the northwest coast, overlooking the Isle of Skye. The second week's thumbprint lies on Nairn, a small town almost directly east of Inverness, on the Moray Firth.

11

Gentle Walks in the Wild Highlands

*E*ven Queen Victoria knew she needed to explore the Highlands at least partly on foot. On her occasional forays from Balmoral Castle, which she carefully recorded in her journals—later published as *Our Life in the Highlands* (1868) and *More Leaves from the Journal of a Life in the Highlands* (1884)—Victoria and her entourage traveled via railway and various horse-drawn conveyances, such as landaus, sociables, and wagonettes. But Victoria also walked.

"At eleven walked out with Beatrice on the road to Kinlochewe, about a mile, and back, greatly admiring the magnificent hills," the queen noted in a journal of her trip to Gairloch Parish in 1877. Despite intermittent rain and unexpected heat, she and her daughter took such an outing almost every day. Like any restless tourist, Victoria liked to get out of her confining carriage: "We drove beyond the habitations to a turn where we could not be overlooked, and scrambled up a bank, where we seated ourselves, and at twenty minutes to three took our luncheon with good appetite. . . . We two remained sketching, for the view was beautiful."

The views near Gairloch, on the northwest coast of Scotland in Wester Ross, are still beautiful, and the best way to see them is still on foot. Anyone who merely drives through the Highlands is apt to become a little blurry. The car window frames mile after mile of forbidding dark mountains, deep sea lochs, wild inland rivers, or *burns*, hillsides covered with conifer plantations, and boggy moors of heather and bracken. The grand scenery rolls by like a jumbled travel film, a soundless *National Geographic* special.

So, like Queen Victoria, James and I knew we would want to get out of the carriage. Walking is one of the main reasons to visit the Highlands anyway, for unlike most of England, this part of Scotland boasts no major cities, a very short list of grand houses, a few far-flung gardens, and a scattering of ruined castles.

When we turned down a deep wooded drive toward Arrow-dale, our rented house near Badachro, just outside Gairloch on the jagged, mountainous coastline overlooking the Isle of Skye, I knew we had chosen well. Arrowdale was a rambling white stone house nestled in its own garden. From the cheerful living room, with its coal-burning fireplace and cushiony chairs, we could look out a huge window at a scooped-out inlet of Loch Gairloch. Hovering above the inlet were soft green hills; behind those, gray eroded mountains with heather-covered lower slopes.

After carefully perusing our local guidebooks and Ordnance Survey maps, we began our week of exploration. Our easiest and certainly most flowery walk was within the vast grounds of Inverewe, Scotland's most celebrated garden, just outside the town of Poolewe, a twenty-minute drive from Gairloch. Paths crisscross the sixty-four-acre site, leading into dells and rock gardens, through groves of rhododendron, and among many rare subtropical plants, protected on this once-barren peninsula by a carefully planted shelter belt of Scots pine and by the Gulf Stream.

Following one path, James and I found ourselves at the edge of the cultivated part of the garden, in front of a tall wooden gate leading into a pine woods. When we unfastened the gate and slipped through, we had no idea where the path would take us. Winding through the woods, we soon emerged on the open shore of Loch Ewe, the saltwater inlet whose deep waters gleamed an almost painfully bright blue under an uncharacteristically sunny sky.

Clambering along the path, now a beaten trail through tall bracken and purple heather, we hung close to the rocky shoreline. Across the loch, although I could see a few clustered houses, the horizon ended in an unbroken line of heather-covered hills. Devoid of trees or any sign of human habitation, these stark hills closed us off from anything beyond water and sky. This atmosphere of remoteness, of separation from an everyday world, was one we were to experience often during our week. Even here, at a well-known garden with tour buses parked at its entrance, the Highlands seemed a place apart.

After startling three fat seals on an offshore rock, who swam around for a long time, staring at us, as if unused to the sight of humans, we reluctantly turned back. On the way home we saw several other footpaths, one of which struck boldly across the foothills into the mountain range that encircles Loch Maree. Two climbers, with packs on their backs and what looked like Alpine boots on their feet, were just disappearing out of sight. I knew they would reach Loch Maree in a few hours, but I had the irrational notion that they were heading into an untracked wilderness.

The next morning, after a home-cooked breakfast of Scots

porridge in front of the bright-red Aga that heated our kitchen, we donned our own version of hiking gear—comfortable walking shoes and rainproof parkas—and set off for two very different walks. Since the morning was once again sunny (James complained that week that we never really saw the renowned Scottish rain), we stopped at a promontory outside Gairloch. It was a viewpoint for Loch Gairloch, and, in the distance, the misty Isle of Skye. Just below the promontory stretched an expanse of curving white sand in a wide scoop of bay.

Scrambling down the rocks for a short walk on the beach, we were lucky enough to see a wild sea otter dash from the dunes, sprint all the way to the water, and dive in. Once safely in the loch, he lolled on his back for a while, watching us, as had the seals, with what seemed like cautious curiosity. From red deer (which we glimpsed a week later in the far north) to sea creatures, wildlife in the Highlands almost seemed—as it probably is—more abundant than people.

Our destination was an inland loch set high in the desolate hills above Loch Ewe, not far from Aultbea. Leaving the main coastal highway, we edged up a narrow lane to a parking area at an isolated hotel high on a hill. Soon we had passed through a gate onto a rough stony track, full of mud holes and puddles, that led through a moorland pasture even higher into the hills. Before long, we were out of sight of hotel, Aultbea, and a sprawling NATO installation, an incongruous intrusion of chain-link fences and modern shedlike buildings that were rare signs we'd seen near Gairloch of economic development.

Within half an hour, this path brought us into a moonscape. All around us were tumbled, glaciated hills with barren crests of gray, lichen-covered rocks rising like islands from a broken sea of purple heather. At the top of one hill we looked down on an unexpected gray sheet of water framed by grassy slopes. No trees or shrubs softened its rock-strewn shoreline. The wide loch curved beyond a hill and disappeared in the distance.

Except for the slight sound of gentle waves as a breeze swept across the loch, and the burble of an occasional stream on the hillside, everything was silent. We heard no birds and saw no waterfowl. The surface of the water was unbroken. The sun had now gone in, leaving a pale mist hanging in the air. We talked in low voices, though no one could have heard us for miles.

For another hour we walked beneath the silent rocky hills, following the shore of the meandering loch. Though unbelievably bleak, this was also strangely beautiful country, with its rugged shapes softened by autumnal tones of gray, purple, dusky green, and the varying russets of bracken. Although it had no human scale or feel to it, I somehow was comforted—in a world becoming so thoroughly tamed and colonized—by its sheer resistance to assimilation.

Although not all our Highland walks felt so uncannily remote, we always had a sense of unfettered space and solitude. Every day, when we set out for a walk, we were alone within minutes. When we decided to search out a specially marked trail starting from the shores of Loch Maree, a steep-sided loch famed for its beauty, I was sure we'd have company, for the trail was described in several guidebooks. But we soon left behind the small group of tourists who had gathered instead at a lochside picnic spot.

Part of a nature reserve, the trail at Loch Maree climbs sharply up the side of Beinn Eighe, a mountain rare in Scotland for retaining some vestiges of its Caledonian pine wood-land. Most of the stark gray crags in the Highlands were long ago stripped for timber, then further denuded by grazing sheep and deer. As their soil became more acid, heather and bracken moved onto the lower slopes, but the tops of these mountains remain cruelly bare. That is why Beinn Eighe, with its woods, is now a landmark.

As the trail passed through bogland, then birch, alder, rowan, willow, and holly as well as pine, views opened out over Loch Maree, which is also remarkable for being still forested on portions of its banks. Towering over Loch Maree, the peak of Slioch dominated the mass of mountains. (Later that week, we thought again of Slioch, when we hiked to a crash site some miles away. See Chapter Seventeen, "Two Scottish War Memorials.")

Scottish weather is famously capricious, and that morning, though mostly sunny, it was playful. Under swiftly moving clouds, the lake and mountains changed character moment to moment. Sometimes the sun shone on a swath of purple heather, then the hillsides sank into a pearly gray. It was as if a watercolorist kept discarding one palette and trying another.

Queen Victoria never hiked this trail to enjoy the pano-ramic views of Loch Maree, but she loved the loch. She stayed by its shores several nights, and she eagerly tried her own hand at capturing the lakeside scenery in watercolors. Her visit is reverently commemorated by a plaque in Gaelic set in front of the Loch Maree Hotel, where passing visitors can still stop and refresh themselves with a pint or a dram.

After a morning on the Beinn Eighe trail, followed by a two-hour hike along another rocky, dark, and wooded path beside the lake, we, too, sought refuge at the venerable Victorian hotel. Like most hotels in Scotland, the Loch Maree Hotel offers bar meals, simple hot dishes or sandwiches served in a cozy, publike room. The bar was somewhat dustily adorned with mounted fish, hoary record-breakers that often dated back to Victoria's day. I wondered if, like us, she had been fortified by the hotel's *Gairloch smokie*, smoked haddock in a rich onion sauce, served with chips and sweet cider.

Some of our excursions around Gairloch were simple ones. After supper we often took a half-hour stroll down the road from our house, sometimes to an old Victorian shooting lodge, now a dignified and somewhat stuffy hotel, and sometimes past a field with a few shaggy Highland cattle and, a bit farther on, a small loch with a moored fishing boat. Wherever we walked, only a few cars passed us, on their way back and forth from the minuscule villages that cling to the lonely coastline south of Badachro. But usually the road might well have been a paved footpath—it wasn't much wider than some—leading to more heather, more mountains, more ocean.

On our last day we drove south as far as we could, all the way to Redpoint, a handful of houses near a seasonal fishing station, about seven miles south of Badachro. At Redpoint the road ends, and only a footpath continues for six miles to a primitive hostel. Looking for the path, we tramped through damp sheep pastures to the edge of the sea, where we finally found a barely discernible trail winding among tufts of grass and clumps of heather.

For three hours we struggled up and down, the sea washing loudly below against cliffs. As we plunged into occasional boggy patches, scaled rocks, and crunched over burgeoning heather, we had to keep searching for traces of our path through grasses bent by the constant seafront winds. We paused often to look not only at our stumbling feet but also at the surging ocean just below us, today an iron color flecked with white surf, and then across the gray water to the misty shape of Skye. I was always aware that week of Skye, dark and indistinct, a constant presence on the horizon.

When we got back to our car, our faces were raw with mist and salt, and my legs ached a little. On this last walk we had been reminded—with comparative gentleness—of what the Highland farmers, shepherds, and fishermen had to face as a daily condition of their life in this harsh landscape.

But the fierceness of this highland world is part of its appeal, and by the end of our week, I knew we would someday be back. On our map we could see more hidden lochs, more footpaths into the roadless interior, more rough tracks along the shore to scattered houses and remote villages. We had only just begun to sample the pleasures of quiet walks in the wild Highlands.

"Have enjoyed this beautiful spot and glorious scenery very much," Queen Victoria remarked in her journal the day before she left Loch Maree and Gairloch Parish. Although the next morning she noted typical West Scotland weather—"A wet, misty morning, no hills whatever to be seen"—she was still sorry to go. "Got up early and breakfasted at half-past eight, and at a quarter to nine we left with regret." On our own last morning in Gairloch, we knew just how she felt.

A FEW FLOATING FACTS

Remember to omit the prefix "0" from an English telephone number when calling from the United States.

We found our rental cottage in the Scottish Tourist Board's publication *Scotland Self-Catering*, obtainable in America for about $12 at some bookstores and through the British Tourist Authority, 551 Fifth Avenue, Suite 701, New York, NY 10176. You may wish to contact the Scottish Tourist Board directly at 23 Ravelston Terrace, Edinburgh, Scotland EH4 3EU, telephone 0131-332-2433, fax 0131-343-1513.

For an informed week's walking, you will need both guidebooks and detailed, large-scale, Ordnance Survey maps. Virtually every small community in Scotland has a shop that sells them (together with postcards, fudge, shortbread, and tiny bottles of Scotch whisky). What we acquired was *Gairloch and Ullapool Area* in the Landranger series, showing our neighborhood at a scale of one-and-a-quarter-inch to one mile, and marking every footpath, lane, and road—not to mention lochs, burns, monuments, houses, even public telephones.

The only kind of guidebook useful for our kind of walking is strictly local, so we headed immediately to the Gairloch Tourist Information Centre. *Walks in Wester Ross*, a paperback by Mary Welsh (about $9), describes in detail forty-five circular walks along the northwest coast, including about fifteen within a half-hour's drive. Two pamphlets thin enough to fold in one's pocket, *Short Walks Around Gairloch* and *Poolewe to Gruinard, Selected Walks and Caves* by Steve Chadwick (each about $3.75), include twenty-three more walks.

Both authors advise on the length of each walk (from a half mile to twelve miles), its difficulty, twists and turns, and associated local history and legend. Chadwick mentions a ruined stone cottage just off the footpath from Poolewe to Kernsary, for example; the site is reputed to be haunted. ("On one occasion a Poolewe man had stopped here and a ghostly figure got into the back of his car. Driving on down the track, he stopped at the gate and the ghost got out to helpfully open it. The driver didn't wait to pick him up!") On a headland near Opinan is the Cave of Gold, where a piper once led a party of children, never to return. "It is said," Chadwick added, "if you listen quietly, you can still hear the piper far away." Who could resist such enticements?

12

Quiet Surprises in the Northeast Highlands

A tidy seaside resort with amusement arcades and a deluxe golf course, a white sweep of curving beach, and a small, snug yacht harbor, all not far from a celebrated New Age spiritual center: this was not exactly how I'd envisioned the wild and rugged Scottish Highlands. When James and I turned into the High Street of Nairn, a town of ten thousand just fifteen miles east of Inverness on the Moray Firth, it seemed almost too civilized.

But this small section of the vast Highlands had more than enough surprises in store. Our first unexpected pleasure was our home for the week, The Round House, a comfortable two-bedroom holiday flat with television, dishwasher, and microwave. What we valued most, however, were its views.

Part of a new development fronting the old harbor, this second-story, curved flat opened onto a marina and a long, handsome pier designed by Thomas Telford in 1820. (Among other engineering feats, Telford supervised the construction of the Caledonian Canal connecting the North Sea and the Atlantic Ocean.) Beyond the marina, we looked far out to sea, flanked on the west by the Black Isle, a peninsula on the other side of the Moray Firth.

A few steps from the flat, across a bridge over the Nairn River, a firm sand beach and wide tidal flat stretched into a hazy distance. Under an overcast sky, the miles of sand shone with an almost iridescent pearly light. In twenty minutes, we could be so far down this empty beach that Nairn almost disappeared from sight. The everyday world was gone too; all we could hear was the faint ripple of water as the tide slid in or out.

Behind this tidal flat rose waves of dunes, and then Culbin Forest, a green darkness looming along the shore. The forest was also once a land of sand and dunes. In 1695, the now-vanished village of Culbin sank under a great sandstorm; legend says that in severe windstorms, shifting sands can still reveal traces of the buried town. Seventy years ago, the Forestry Commission began to plant Corsican pines to stabilize Culbin Sands, and now a complex network of paths crisscrosses a tall, dense, and almost impenetrable woods. On the morning we explored part of Culbin Forest, we carefully noted each turn of the path on our map. We did not want to lose our way under those silent marching pines.

If we left our front door and headed west instead of east, we immediately turned onto a seafront promenade. This long paved path ran for more than two miles past shops, houses, and a few grand hotels, taking advantage of the magnificent panorama of the Moray Firth. The paved path mediated between clipped green lawns and flowering gardens on one side, crashing surf on the other.

On our first Sunday in Nairn, we joined the promenade on the paved path: young families and their strollers, boys and girls on bikes, older men and women with canes, and a genial group of other walkers out to enjoy a sunny, if windy, morning. Every few minutes we stepped off the path to make room for red-faced, puffing runners, who were just finishing the last laps of a triathlon. Though newly arrived tourists, we felt we had suddenly stepped that morning into the community life of Nairn.

Although we did not spend much of our time in Nairn itself, we enjoyed its small-town atmosphere. Many towns in Britain are losing their main-street traffic to supermarkets and even mini-malls, but Nairn's High Street seemed to be still thriving. We quickly decided on a favorite butcher, who made his own chicken-and-mushroom pot pies, sausage rolls, and individual quiches daily, and a baker, whose large, sunny window advertised Clava bread, a heavy round loaf named after the nearby prehistoric Clava Cairns.

From the local tourist information center we purchased two invaluable pamphlets: *Walks Around and About Nairn*, which described and mapped ten outings of about an hour each, and *From Nairn to Loch Ness* by Edward Meldrum, an astonishingly detailed account of local history and archaeology. Meldrum knew every farm, standing stone, chapel, ruin, bridge—and more—between Nairn and Inverness.

We had time to sample only a small part of one of his suggested routes; his guidebook led us painstakingly through central Nairn, dating and describing every building and monument, even those now vanished. ("In front is the Market Cross, renovated 1757, a circular stone pillar capped by a square head, once a sundial known as the Horologe Stone.")

Although Nairn itself was charming, with narrow streets and low picturesque cottages near its old harborside Fishertown, we liked it best because it was so close to intriguing walks and excursions, all within a half-hour's drive or less.

Despite our nearness to Inverness, we preferred to explore the countryside.

Our first foray was to Findhorn, a tiny resort known for water sports, about fifteen miles east along the coast. As an avid gardener, I had read about the extraordinarily large flowers and vegetables once grown by three individuals who started a garden on the Findhorn dunes in 1962. Their spiritual explorations and adventures eventually led to the forming of the Findhorn Foundation. Now an internationally known New Age community of about two hundred, housed in an expanding group of buildings just outside the village, the foundation offers year-round courses, lectures, and conferences.

For casual visitors like us, much of Findhorn's grounds are open to view, as are a visitor information center, store, coffee shop, and a nearby large garden (with healthy-looking but normal-size plants). Occasional guided tours are also available. We strolled briefly along the pleasant paths, watched community members moving purposefully to their barracks or offices, read bulletin-board notices about shiatsu massage and yoga, and listened with surprise to several American accents, the only ones we heard all week. Findhorn seemed as if it could easily be transplanted to the northern coast of California.

But when we left the foundation and drove a mile to the dunes on Burghead Bay, we were immediately reminded that we were in northern Scotland. A fierce wind was blowing that day—"the equinoctial gales," a television weatherman claimed—and we almost could not stand up on the strip of shingle beach. Waves were smashing against the shore, which curved miles along the coast back toward Nairn. No one else was on this deserted beach—except for a man in a black wetsuit who was steadying his sailboard in the fuming surf.

As we watched, both horrified and fascinated, he leapt on the board and soared straight out to sea. We could not believe that he could even stay on the board in such a gale. In moments, the wind had carried him almost beyond our sight. Then, just as we were sure he was a goner, he turned on a knife-edge, and the wind hurled him swiftly back to shore, where he slid off his board as if he'd just had an agreeable ride. That display of courage and skill, against the wildly inhospitable background of sea and sky, seemed somehow peculiarly Scottish.

On our way home from Findhorn, we took a brief detour from the New Age to prehistory. Turning off the main road at Forres, a town six miles south of Findhorn, we stopped to admire Sueno's Stone, a carved twenty-foot sandstone slab covered on all sides with foliage, beasts, and rows of warriors. Dating from the ninth century, it is an unexplained legacy of the mysterious Picts. Now this massive stone stands in a glassed protective enclosure next to a very modern housing development on the outskirts of Forres, a juxtaposition that catches the anomalies of contemporary Scotland.

Not every exhilarating walk near Nairn has to be by the sea. A few days later, we sought out another Findhorn. Deep in the hilly countryside south of Nairn, the Findhorn River winds tortuously toward the coast. Tracing our way carefully on our large-scale Ordnance Survey Landranger map, we parked next to Daltulich Bridge, an almost indiscernible landmark on a very minor road, and passed through an opening in a low wall. Then, just as the Nairn leaflet on walks promised, we were suddenly on a well-kept footpath through the trees high above the rushing river.

For more than an hour we walked along the Findhorn, looking far down on the peat-brown, white-flecked water. As the path curved and climbed higher, we would sometimes emerge onto a rocky outcrop that gave us dramatic perspectives up and across the steep wooded gorge. Below us, the water swept and swirled over heaped boulders, crashed down short falls, and lapped into deep pools. Sun glinted on the foaming dark water and through the filtering canopy of leaves. The path seemed almost magical. Except for one fisherman and his *ghillie*, or guide, we saw no one all the way to Randolph's Leap, a precipitous narrowing of the river overlooked by high stone shelves.

Taking a wrong turn on the way home along a maze of minor roads, we ended our afternoon with an unexpected visit to the Ardclach Bell Tower. This is a two-story tower house, built in 1655, once used for both a local jail and watchtower, as well as a belfry. To see the tower, a visitor stops along the quiet road some distance away, takes out a large key from an honor-system glass box on a post, drives to the foot of a hill, and ascends what seem like hundreds of steep steps. Although the interior of the tower was dark and clammy—not a place to linger, even in a sudden shower—the hilltop was isolated and peaceful, and the views were panoramic, over valley, hills, and another curve of the Findhorn River.

Larger and grander towers were not hard to find, since several of Scotland's most famous preserved castles are within a half-hour's drive of Nairn. South of Nairn, Cawdor Castle is spacious, handsome, and well done up, down to the cheerful strips of tartan carpeting laid for tourists. Begun toward the end of the fourteenth century, the castle, like most fortified houses, was gradually expanded and altered. Aside from its antique furniture, tapestries, and artwork, Cawdor offered two unexpected delights.

One was the pamphlet of "room notes," written with great style and wit by Lord Cawdor. His irreverent humor reminded us how stuffy most great-house guidebooks are. Pointing out two Chippendale four-posters, for example, he comments: "The beds are not identical twins but even so, together, they form an undistinguished, amiable, English couple." On a locomotive nameplate: "This note is for railway enthusiasts only, so pigeon-fanciers should press on regardless." His ancestors do not escape his wry attentions: "The enormously overgrown sampler was worked by another indefatigable Campbell aunt, Lady Muriel Boyle. . . . Of the six pictures, the lady like a cassowary who presides at the top is Dame Campbell of Clunas."

Since I have often puzzled over Latin inscriptions, trying to recall my long-lost rudiments of that language, I snickered happily at Lord Cawdor's comment on a stone fireplace in the dining room: "The allegorical design and the inscription in dog Latin have never been satisfactorily explained or translated, all of which is highly satisfactory. The writing may mean 'In the morning, remember your creators.' Or it may mean something quite else, like 'If you stay too long in the evening, you will remember it in the morning.' "

The other pleasure Cawdor offers in abundance is walking. After a stroll through the extensive garden, we had to choose among a variety of paths through its woodlands. Our two-and-a-half-mile route led along a rapidly flowing stream, past tall beech trees, and through shady, half-open groves. As on our other walks, we found ourselves alone. Most of the visitors to Cawdor come to see only the castle, drawn by its half-familiar name. It is one of the settings of Shakespeare's *Macbeth*, although as Lord Cawdor remarks: "The truth is that as

Cawdor Castle was not built until the late fourteenth century, it is impossible for King Duncan to have lost any blood or Lady Macbeth much sleep in this particular house."

Like Cawdor, Brodie Castle, a few miles east of Nairn, also had a striking plain angularity, a sort of stern abstraction, on the outside, and a surprising amount of comfort and decoration on the inside, including a lavishly wrought plasterwork ceiling, dating from the seventeenth century, in the dining room.

"There have been Brodies at Brodie for over 800 years," its conventional guidebook rather dauntingly announces, and the current tenant, Brodie of Brodie, was standing guard in the drawing room on the afternoon we visited. Not many tourists were passing through that day, and his post looked rather boring. James and I were glad we were free to escape to the grounds, where, as at Cawdor, several walks beckoned, especially one that curved around a small marshy lake.

Our last castle, Castle Stuart, was west of Nairn. It, too, was still inhabited, but by paying guests; begun in 1621, the dignified tall tower house was recently restored and now serves as a discreet, luxurious hotel—or, as the brochure suggests, "Accommodation Available by Appointment." Visitors can also take a guided tour of the castle and hear some of the castle's history, as well as several suitably chilling ghost stories. I rather liked the current excitements: the local bank manager had recently been married in the salon, the castle's first wedding in three hundred years, and a Japanese troop of Highland dancers—the Japanese Bluebells—had lately performed on the newly varnished floor of the great hall.

On the way home to Nairn for supper that evening, I kept thinking about those incongruous Japanese Highland dancers.

As I went back over our day in my mind, they curtsied and pointed, dipped and jigged, in tartans that recalled the carpets of the venerable Cawdor and Brodie castles. It was just this mixture of tradition and surprise, I decided, that had made our stay in Nairn so rewarding.

A FEW FLOATING FACTS

Remember to omit the prefix "0" from an English telephone number when calling from the United States. Prices are calculated at $1.60 to the pound.

We found the Round House in the Scottish Tourist Board's publication *Scotland Self-Catering*, obtainable in America for about $12 at some bookstores and through the British Tourist Authority, 551 Fifth Avenue, Suite 701, New York, NY 10176. You may wish to contact the Scottish Tourist Board directly at 23 Ravelston Terrace, Edinburgh, Scotland EH4 3EU, telephone 0131-332-2433, fax 0131-343-1513.

An elegant if expensive place to pause for lunch or dinner during outings from Nairn is the Culloden House Hotel, associated with Bonnie Prince Charlie and his final battle at nearby Drumossie Moor. It is a handsome mansion set in several acres of well-tended parkland, located three miles from Inverness, off the A96, telephone 01463-790461. Less costly than dinner, a two-course lunch with coffee afterward (complete with freshly baked shortbread), including tax and tip, was £12.99 (about $21) in 1995.

Perched at little tables overlooking the oceanfront, we also enjoyed an unpretentious bar lunch at the Golf View Hotel in

Nairn. A ham-and-cheese omelette accompanied by a salad garnish and ubiquitous chips (french fries), with a glass of sweet cider, was £8 ($12.80).

We learned about both these restaurants from an invaluable paperback, *Taste of Scotland* (in 1995, £4.50 or $7.20), which lists and describes a selected group of recommended places at which to eat and stay, ranging from five-star hotels to farmhouses. This guide is hard to find; I faxed a credit card number and ordered it mailed to our first address in Scotland. In 1995, the guide sent air mail to the United States cost £8 ($12.80). Taste of Scotland Scheme Ltd., 33 Melville Street, Edinburgh EH3 7JF, telephone 0131-220-1900, fax 0131-220-6102.

III

Special Places

WESTERN
ISLES
AREA

Gairloch
Loch Maree

SKYE

HIGHLANDS

MULL

JURA

ISLAY

SCOTLAND

Aberdeen

North Sea

Edinburgh

North Atlantic Ocean

Newcastle upon Tyne

LAKE DISTRICT

ISLE OF MAN

Irish Sea

ANGLESEY

York

SNOWDONIA

ENGLAND

North Norfolk Coast

WALES

Stratford-upon-Avon

London

Ashdown Forest

Lynmouth & Lynton

Hartfield

EXMOOR

Wakehurst Place

BODMIN MOOR

Standen

DARTMOOR

Heaven Farm

Strait of Dover

St. Michael's Mount

English Channel

N

0   100 km

0   100 miles

A Note on Special Places

"What is your favorite place in all of England?" I never know how to answer this question. As soon as I think of one special place, another one flashes into my mind, and then another. It is as if all my trips to England were on an unedited film that begins automatically playing whenever I picture any part of the English countryside (or any street or park in London). I try to zoom in close, but suddenly I find myself looking at another frame.

What about the northwest coast of Cornwall, near Bude? Perhaps, specifically, Sandymouth Bay? But do I really love that place more than the genteel seaside resorts in Devon, or the windblown dunes of the North Norfolk coast, not to mention the high moorland cliffs of Exmoor that plunge down to the sea? Did I say cliffs? How could I forget the mountains of the Lake District? Or the gardens of Kent and Sussex? The South Downs? The Yorkshire Dales?

And so the film pulls me from place to place, and the person who asked such a seemingly simple question—"What is your favorite place?"—has probably given up and gone away.

In the following section I give at least a sampling of some of my favorite places in England (and two special places in Scotland). If I had written even a short chapter on each of the other places I remember vividly and affectionately, this would not be a guidebook, but an encyclopedia.

13

St. Michael's Mount:
A Fairy-Tale Castle

On our first trip to Cornwall, when I saw on our map a turret-shaped symbol called St. Michael's Mount, I was prepared to be disappointed. Although I had not then been to the fabled Mont St. Michel in France, Henry Adams's *Mont St. Michel and Chartres* had created for me a sense of its awesome presence. I was skeptical about England's much smaller counterpart, which certainly had a less mellifluous name. My husband, who had traveled in France, added to my doubts: "Oh, yes, Mont St. Michel. Very impressive, but everything around it is awfully tacky. Souvenir shops and stalls everywhere. Crowds of people, tour buses, noise."

But I have retained a small child's fascination with castles and nurtured a lifelong love of islands. How could I possibly resist a castle built on an island in the sea? I drew a red circle on the map offshore at Marazion, near Penzance, and we deflected our course. As we neared Marazion the next day, I noted in one of my British guidebooks that this area was "a spot for holidaymakers" and, according to another, "a crowded vacation mecca." I began to picture ice cream stands, candy shops, postcard kiosks, hawkers of T-shirts and beanies, hordes of sightseers.

So when we rounded a turn in the road and first saw St. Michael's Mount, I caught my breath in delighted surprise. A wide beach curved around the bay, whose bright waters glittered in the sun. In the middle of the bay, a precipitous hill, rocky but with green cultivated terraces, rose from the water. Atop the hill was a medieval castle, gabled and turreted, of weathered gray-brown stone. It looked like a fairy-tale mountain in *From the Tower Window*, one of my favorite childhood books.

On this mild June day, the beach was uncrowded. A few refreshment stands and a carousel only added a good-natured holiday air to the inviting stretch of sand. Since it was close to four o'clock, the last of the day's sunseekers were already folding their towels and furling their umbrellas, heading homeward for tea or supper. A small motor launch hovering by a long seawall waited for scarce tourists. Paying the equivalent of two dollars, we hopped aboard. Brief as the ride was, it gave us a whiff of salt air and the satisfying slap of waves against the side of the putt-putting boat.

Once on the island, we passed a series of unobtrusive outbuildings—kept pristine by the National Trust, which administers the Mount—and began a slow walk up stone slabs, so wide they seemed like steps fit for a giant, that led to the castle. Thousands of pilgrims, then soldiers, and finally families with children had climbed these steps. Originally St. Michael's Mount was a Benedictine abbey, founded in 1135 as a subsidiary of Mont St. Michel. Later it became an important fortress. Since 1659, the Mount has been the seat of the St. Aubyn family, who still live there. (A hundred years ago, Sir John St. Aubyn became the first Lord St. Levan.)

Like many of England's great houses, the Mount feels like a

home, not a museum. On my first trip to Europe, many years
ago, when I eagerly entered a romantic-looking German
castle, I found it cold, damp, and smelling of mildew. St.
Michael's Mount is, in contrast, almost warm and welcoming.
Wandering virtually alone through the castle (discreet guards
sat quietly in each room), we sensed the unseen presence of
past and present inhabitants. Though the rooms were filled
with furniture, paintings, and memorabilia, they were neither
grandiose nor overpowering.

A long family history is evident everywhere. Our printed
guide informed us of Sir John's Room that it "has long been
used as the private sitting-room of the owner of the Mount." I
thought the owner probably also used the little Library (for-
merly the Breakfast Room) as well, for it invited browsing
among its simple pine bookshelves. Set on rich but subdued
Oriental carpets, overstuffed crimson armchairs waited for
someone to sink into them, and a cushioned window nook offered two more seats for cozy reading. The smoking room,
gaily painted with a light turquoise wash, was the butler's
serving room until 1877, when an oriel window was added.
Then it became a comfortable retreat for Victorian gentle-
men, who came here for cigars and port after dinner. Now
thoroughly in the mood, I could easily picture myself in a silk
dressing gown, sitting in the corner with a book beneath the
oriel window.

Even the grandest room, called Chevy Chase, was not
daunting. Named for a seventeenth-century plaster frieze
whose lively figures and animals enact scenes from a medieval
ballad, this room was once the monks' refectory. Today it still
serves as a dining room, dominated by a huge gleaming oak
table dating from the early 1600s, and twelve massive chairs

that are models of those used by the monks. The deep brown curves of a restored timbered ceiling make the upper part of the room almost seem like the carefully crafted hull of a Tudor ship.

But, like the rest of the castle, Chevy Chase is not oppressively austere. Its polished oak floor was laid in 1723, when local ladies requested the current St. Aubyn to provide a suitable dancing space. A hundred years ago, another St. Aubyn had bits of centuries-old painted and enameled Flemish glass set into the leaded windows. Now, when shafts of light strike those flecks of warm color, the windows shimmer with subdued brilliance. Shifting my picture from black-robed monks, sitting silently in a timbered room, to brocaded ladies in powdered wigs, tripping the light fantastic, I left Chevy Chase with renewed appreciation for the confident but respectful way the English can alter historic buildings to keep them vibrantly alive.

Emerging into the sunshine, James and I stood on a stone terrace roof that forms part of the large Victorian wing of the castle. Peering over the wall, we saw gardens below, filled with bright color and tropical plants the brochure assured us were not often found in England. Terraced lawns below the garden fell sharply to an extensive gray rocky ledge, perfect for clambering and sunning, that in turn sank by stages, changing color like a chameleon, into the blue-green water. Beyond was a splash of tossing sea and cloud-sprinkled sky, with Penzance far in the distance.

Beneath us were five floors of private family quarters, not open to the public. Just then, as I leaned over the parapet, I heard the laughter of children. I could barely glimpse around the corner a wide bay window opening out onto the same view. Two small children were playing in the window seat. I wondered what it might be like to look out daily on the sea from that bay window, so high up, watching storms gather and clouds race across the sky, hearing the fierce Atlantic gales break against the thick stone walls, and riding above the waves in that sheltered room. How would it be to entertain guests on this terrace? To walk on sunny days in the gardens far below? To catch a tan on those accessible rocky ledges?

Pleasant and comfortable as the Mount seems, however, it still retains an air of mystery. From the terrace, a visitor leaves the domestic castle and enters in a moment the world of the great Benedictine abbeys. Small but impressive, the Priory Church, founded on the rock that forms the summit of the island, contains both family pews and space for public worship services. Its fifteenth-century rose windows cast a soft glow over the much-restored interior.

But the church holds darker memories as well. Under the family pews on the right, a sharp, narrow stone stair lurches steeply into forbidding blackness. This was once the castle's dungeon. Peering down the stairs, I shivered. While those in power walked on the sunny ledges, others obviously languished in the cold darkness below. Our brochure cryptically noted: "During the last century, a skeleton of a man over seven feet tall was found in it. No one knows who he was nor why he was imprisoned here." I remembered the giant-size stone steps that led up to the castle, and the legend of Jack the Giant Killer, long associated with the Mount. But that skeleton, no doubt bleached and covered with dirt, was no fairy tale. It was salutary to be reminded that neither was this great castle. A repository of all kinds of human history, it had seen far more than praying monks and dancing ladies.

St. Michael's Mount has also tolerated a certain amount of human idiosyncrasy. The English often cherish their domestic oddities, and the St. Aubyns had enshrined a few of their own. After leaving the church, we passed through the elegant eighteenth-century Blue Drawing Rooms, created from the ruins of a Lady Chapel, into the Map Room. What caught my attention in the Map Room were not just the antique maps of Cornwall displayed on the walls. I was drawn to several pieces of historic detritus that seemed to have inexplicably washed up there: a faded handkerchief, a small cork model of the castle, and the remains of a cat.

The handkerchief, hung in a glazed frame, was reputed to have belonged to Oliver Cromwell, and, as the brochure proudly noted, had been preserved here for over three centuries. Looking at this clean and pressed handkerchief (did Cromwell ever blow in it?), I wondered, as I sometimes do, about what we choose to venerate and why. My musings wandered further as I studied the miniature Mount, which had been meticulously constructed by an early twentieth-century butler from discarded corks of champagne bottles. (When did he find time to do this? How much champagne did all those corks represent? Did the butler ever secretly wish he could have been an architect? What did all this say, if anything, about the English class system?) By the time I got to the cat, a wrapped oblong parcel labeled as an Egyptian mummy, my questions turned to smothered giggles. What was this mummified cat doing in the Map Room? What sort of tourist would bring such a thing home as a souvenir? Was this leathery relic the ultimate expression of the English passion for pets?

The last stop on our self-guided tour of the Mount fortunately took us back to the sunshine. In the 1870s, an architecturally inclined St. Aubyn designed a stone dairy, modeled after one at Glastonbury Abbey, to process milk from the small herd of Jersey cows then kept on the island. Inside this small, airy, and charming building, with its mellowed wood tables and shelves, large clean pottery bowls, and shining copper fittings, I might not have minded being—though very briefly—a dairymaid.

From a mysterious skeleton to a mummified cat, an ancient chapel to a Georgian drawing room, a sunny terrace to a gun battery, St. Michael's Mount held in its fairly small compass more records of English life and history than I could absorb. I tried to imagine the astonished fishermen who, according to an old Cornish legend, saw the Archangel St. Michael standing on a rocky ledge on the western side of the Mount. Later saints came here, too, and so did an emissary from Isolde's husband, King Mark, who wanted to buy from the Mount fine clothes of wool, silk, and linen for his bride, whose tragic love for Tristan was her undoing.

In the thirteenth century, the church on the Mount was destroyed by an earthquake and rebuilt a hundred years later. During the Middle Ages, many pilgrims sought out the shrine of St. Michael, and it became an important stop on the main highway through Cornwall. In 1588 the beacon on the church tower signaled the approach of the Spanish Armada. Whenever internal wars threatened England, the Mount was fiercely defended, captured, regained, lost, sold. After visiting the area in 1937, Von Ribbentrop, the Nazi foreign minister, reportedly decided to make the Mount his home if the Germans won the war. Earthquakes, sieges, invasions, wars: the tides of English history rose, broke against the rocky shores of the Mount, fell back, and rose again.

At Mount St. Michael, however, history is never irre-deemably gloomy. After descending from the castle, we bought tickets for its gardens. From the castle high above, I had thought they looked attractive. But once among them, I realized how little I had actually seen. The approach led through a wildflower meadow planted with waves of blue-bells, white anemones, and red poker flowers. Then the gar-dens themselves rolled on and on, flowing around the foot of the castle, swooping toward the water. Laid out as a series of steep rooms separated by stairs, hedges, and paths, they were filled with daffodils, tulips, geraniums, daisies in blue, white, and yellow, and exotic blooms I couldn't identify.

Many of the exquisite small terraces held equally tiny shel-ters, where one or two people could sit in seclusion, sur-rounded by flowers, and look at the sea. Flowers, ocean, privacy—I had a flash of envy. "You know how much I love you, James," I said to my husband. "I've never thought of any-one I'd want to leave you for. But if I could live at the Mount and walk every day in these gardens, Lord St. Levan might give me pause."

We were the last tourists to leave the Mount. The tide had gone out, so we could now walk back on a cobbled causeway, as if someone had struck a staff and opened it for us in the middle of the sea. Stepping carefully over the slippery stone path, we turned once to look back at the castle.

Lights were going on in high windows. A fund-raiser was being held tonight, a guide had told us. Before us, at the far end of the causeway, we could see two women walking, jewels glinting in their hair, long satiny gowns brushing the stones. For a moment I almost hoped that they had come in a coach, one that might turn into a pumpkin as magically as the water would soon cover the causeway again, leaving St. Michael's Mount to float once more in the surrounding sea.

A FEW FLOATING FACTS

Prices are calculated at $1.60 to the pound.

St. Michael's Mount, owned by the National Trust, is located at Marazion, a half mile south of A394, near Penzance. It is open from April 1 to October 31, Monday to Friday, ten-thirty to five-thirty, and from November to the end of March, "guided tours or free flow, as tide, weather and circumstances permit; no regular ferry service during this period." Ferries may operate only in favorable boating conditions at any time of year. Access on foot over the causeways at low tide. Admission £3.50 ($5.60), family ticket £9 ($14.40).

The Mount is also open most weekends during the season for special charity days.

Owing to narrow passages within the castle, it may be necessary to restrict visitors. Delays may occur at the height of the season.

The Trust runs a café and restaurant from spring to early fall.

14

Ashdown Forest:
Pooh Country

*I*discovered Winnie-the-Pooh country by accident. Glancing through some tourist brochures while staying in Sussex, I noticed an advertisement for Pooh Corner, a shop in nearby Hartfield that specialized in Winnie-the-Pooh. Reading on, I discovered that Hartfield had been the country home of A. A. Milne, who had set his world-famous children's stories, *Winnie-the-Pooh* and *The House at Pooh Corner*, in adjoining Ashdown Forest.

The Forest! Although it had been years since I had reread the Pooh stories, I did remember the seductive appeal of the Forest. "Once upon a time, a very long time ago now, about last Friday, Winnie-the-Pooh lived in a forest all by himself under the name of Sanders." His friend Christopher Robin had lived, enticingly, "behind a green door in another part of the forest." Neither as child nor adult had I ever stopped to consider whether this Enchanted Place, as Milne called it, really existed.

Although James and I had stayed several times on the very edge of Ashdown Forest, a preserve of 6,400 acres only seventy miles from London, we had never known it was there. Unlike Pooh Corner, Ashdown Forest does not advertise. We had often skirted it without realizing what it was, on our way to the gardens of Kent and Sussex or heading south on the busy A26 toward Brighton. I had noticed that the surrounding countryside seemed very lightly populated, but I had not wondered why.

That countryside is, in fact, part of Ashdown Forest, a wild and beautiful expanse of both damp and dry heathland that encompasses patches of woodland, streams, bogs, farms, and villages. Designated a Site of Special Scientific Interest, the forest is a complex ecosystem, a richly historic landscape, and a parklike refuge for walkers, horseback riders, and picnickers. It is also the dream-tinged land of solitude and freedom created by E. H. Shepard in his illustrations for Milne's stories.

To get a proper introduction to Ashdown Forest, James and I stopped at the Forest Centre, tucked into Broadstone Warren, just past Wych Cross, where the A22 and A275 meet. The centre is housed in three old oak-framed and heather-thatched barns, which the Conservators, a governing body that regulates Ashdown Forest, has re-erected and turned into offices and workshops. The centre offers programs, informative displays, booklets, brochures, and trail maps.

Here we learned that Ashdown Forest began in 1372, when Edward III granted the forest as part of the Manor of Duddleswell to John of Gaunt, Duke of Lancaster. It is part of the Weald, often called "the Garden of England," an area of southeast England described by Nigel Nicolson in *Nigel Nicolson's Kent* as "a district of small villages, few towns, many farms, woods, oast houses and fruit blossoms."

Long a royal hunting preserve of the medieval English kings, Ashdown Forest eventually passed to the Earl De La Warr as Lord of the Manor, who sold it to the East Sussex

County Council. The council in turn set up a trust to administer the forest in perpetuity.

But the forest is, of course, even more ancient. Neolithic man hunted there, and evidence of Iron Age enclosures can be found at several places in the forest. The Romans built and improved trackways to gain access to iron-ore workings. In 731 the Venerable Bede described it as "thick and inaccessible; a place of retreat for large herds of deer and swine," inhabited by wild boars and wolves.

On the early spring day James and I set out from the information center to explore some of the forest, we did not have to worry about either accessibility or ravening beasts. The forest is easy to enter. A sharp-eyed driver can spot many turnoffs along the intersecting roads that cross it, and these parking places lead to paths through the woods or across the heathland.

Although wolves and boars are long gone, the forest is still home to a large protected herd of fallow deer as well as badgers, hedgehogs, foxes, weasels, rabbits, and many other small animals. (In *Ashdown Forest*, a small book obtainable at the Forest Centre, the late naturalist Garth Christian lovingly lists all the forest inhabitants, down to "the delightful little dormouse.")

On our short excursion, we did not see any wildlife. But we did see a vast panorama of land and sky. Our path from the centre led in minutes onto the open heath, and suddenly we found ourselves on the side of an almost bare hill, looking down and across a lightly wooded valley, past scattered farms, and many miles away to other hills—the North Downs—that disappeared into the distance. It was one of those views that convinces me that the English countryside goes on forever.

This was not the Sussex or Kentish farming country I thought I knew, filled with prosperous villages (now often kept up by well-to-do commuting Londoners) and with orchards, productive fields, and lush gardens. This was wild moorland, covered in heather, bracken, and gorse, with a fierce wind blowing over it that promised rain. Although I knew that the road was not far behind us, I felt as if we had been suddenly transported to Exmoor or even to the gentler parts of the Yorkshire moors. Were we really only an hour from London?

The Broadstone Trail, which we were following, leads for two and a half miles past a disused stone quarry (Ashdown sandstone was once used to build local houses), along a stream called Miry Ghyll, across a plank bridge into a wooded valley of mossy plants and ferns, and then across a traditional earth-covered sod bridge back into the heather. With time pressing, we had to omit the part of the trail that led into a small bog via a log causeway. Ashdown Forest continued to surprise us. Not far from the returning path was a familiar close-cropped green expanse, part of the Royal Ashdown Forest Golf Course.

From the Forest Centre we drove in fifteen minutes to Hartfield, a charming village (recently awarded a prize for "Best Kept in Sussex") with a High Street of half-timbered shops and houses. Its medieval church has a fifteenth-century shingled-spire tower looking rather like an elegant peaked hat. At the south end of Hartfield High Street, in a Queen Anne building dating from the 1690s, stands Pooh Corner.

I wondered what Milne and Shepard—both of whom, according to Ann Thwaite, Milne's recent biographer, eventually loathed the little bear's celebrity—would have thought of Pooh Corner. Sixty-odd years after Milne wrote his books, a

Pooh industry now turns out stuffed animals, games, tea towels, sweatshirts, place mats, plastic and china mugs, tins, badges, key rings, rulers, felt-tip pens, swim bags, height charts, counting friezes, name stamps, posters, notebooks, stationery, pop-up books, sticker books, coloring books, scrapbooks, and an infinite number of greeting cards.

Would Milne have exercised his gentle irony on the ingenuity of *Pooh's Busy Day Pad: A Collection of Pooh-ish Things to Colour, Cut Out and Make Up*, or the four-inch Piglet doll, which has a cloth mini-story attached to its belly, or Stitch-a-Pooh-Picture, with canvas, yarn, and instructions included?

He might well have approved, however, of the staples at Pooh Corner (whose sign also proclaims CHRISTOPHER ROBIN's SWEET SHOP). Lined up on shelves, fifty large glass jars display hard candies with delicious-sounding names, from bull's-eyes (which Christopher Milne notes in his own memoir, *The Enchanted Places*, he loved as a child), to mint eclairs, lemon sherbets, barley sugars, blackberry-and-custards, spearmint chews, Tom Thumb drops, blackcurrant-and-licorice, and forty-one more. Army-and-Navies, grayish-blue drops with a spicy strong flavor, can easily camouflage a cold, according to owner Michael Ridley, who warned, "They are not for the fainthearted." The fainthearted might well prefer the gentler teddy-bear drops, with a texture between a gumdrop and a firm candy, and shaped, of course, like little teddy bears.

In a cheery room at the side of the shop, Pooh Corner also provides refreshments, served on bright white crockery at six tables spread with pink-and-white gingham cloths, under pink and white balloons. Teatime might include a pot of tea, *quosh* (a kind of orange pop or squash), *flapjacks* (oat squares with treacle, not American pancakes), and gingerbread.

Sitting under the balloons, we studied a one-page handout giving directions to Poohsticks Bridge. This, as Milne fans know, is where Winnie-the-Pooh invented the game of Pooh-sticks, when friends each drop a stick on one side of the bridge and then hurry to the other side to see whose stick drifts through first.

Although it had begun to rain, James and I were now determined to explore Pooh's part of the forest. Only minutes away, along the B2026 and then right at Chuck Hatch on a minor road toward Marsh Green and Newbridge, a parking area was conveniently signposted for Poohsticks Bridge. Arrows pointed to the footpath, which led through Posingford Wood. In *The Enchanted Places* Christopher Milne recalls this part of the forest as "a gay and friendly wood, the sort of wood you could happily walk through at night, feeling yourself a skilful rather than a brave explorer: a wood of hazels and willows and sweet chestnuts with here and there an oak or pine."

On a weekday rainy March morning, we were the only pilgrims, but from the generous size of the parking space, and a sign warning of car thieves, we judged that summer would bring plenty of Pooh-seekers. My own ardor for the quest suddenly waned when we came to a bridleway leading sharply downhill to the bridge. Not much more than a sunken ditch edged with barbed-wire fencing, the churned-up bridleway had been thoroughly trodden into mire during the recent rains. After sinking a few steps ankle-deep in muck, I announced that I was willing to take Poohsticks Bridge on faith.

(A year later, back at Ashdown Forest during drier weather, we walked without any difficulty along the downhill path to the bridge. Since no other tourists had evidently begun their

Pooh treks, we stood together in contented silence on the small wooden bridge. Looking over the side down into the narrow, swift stream, which quickly disappeared into a tangled thicket of greening trees and shrubs, we could almost feel the rush of oncoming spring. On this bright cool morning, it was very possible to imagine a young boy, and his Pooh bear, standing here too, watching the water and wondering what lay just out of sight in the depths of Ashdown Forest.)

After circling uphill through pastures and fields along a path that led us beyond the edge of the forest, we reluctantly returned to the parking area. I consulted my Ordnance Survey Landranger map to locate any other Pooh sites. Five-Hundred Acre Wood: wouldn't that be Milne's Hundred-Acre Wood? Off we went, back along the B2026, until another parking area beckoned.

Since the sun had reappeared, we struck onto the nearest path. Climbing a bracken-covered hill, we were suddenly again overlooking the same extensive view (though from a different angle) we had enjoyed at the Forest Centre: green hills in the hazy distance, with houses and farms looking like a set of miniatures dotted here and there. This is where Pooh and Christopher Robin felt "the whole world spread out until it reached the sky."

Just below the top of the hill, crowned by a clump of Scots pines, we saw a small, roughly fenced, overgrown enclosure, almost like an untended burial mound. Inside the enclosure, a plaque had been set into one of several large rocks: "AND BY AND BY THEY CAME TO AN ENCHANTED PLACE ON THE VERY TOP OF THE FOREST CALLED GALLEON'S LAP. Here at Gills Lap are commemorated A. A. Milne (1882–1956) and E. H. Shepard (1879–1976), who collaborated in the creation of Winnie-the-Pooh and so captured the magic of Ashdown Forest and gave it to the world."

From the top of Gills Lap, we could see for miles in every direction, a full circular sweep over the moorland and bits of woods. In early spring, the heathland was still brown and russet, though heather was blooming here and there and wild primroses sparkled along many of the paths. The damp wind blew through the pines with a soft, reassuring swoosh. I could see why Milne, and Christopher Robin, had loved it here.

On the way home, I studied the changing aspects of Ashdown Forest. Trails led onto many heath-covered hills that I had once dismissed as uninteresting and infertile farmland. Pine groves and stands of hardwood trees beckoned on slopes and in valleys. Even on this cool, rainy, off-season morning, a few hikers could be seen in the distance, a casual walker with her dog on a leash, two more serious trekkers with day packs on their back. Hiking Ashdown could turn into quite an expedition: its six thousand acres lead gradually into the South Downs, and the Downs roll then to the sea.

As we drove through Ashdown Forest, I realized that it had yet another face, a familiar one of modest tourist attractions, many of which have prospered in recent years all over England. This Ashdown Forest includes Heaven Farm, once the "home farm" for a nearby estate, Danehurst, and now open to visitors, with farm museum and educational tours. A nature trail of one-and-a-half miles through the farm's surrounding land recently won a Conservation Award from the South of England Agricultural Society. (See Chapter Twenty, "Bluebell Woods," for more on Heaven Farm.)

Ashdown Forest Farm, also a family-run working farm, has a collection of farm animals with appeal to children, like

Ben, the miniature Shire horse; sheep who roam free around the farmyard; goats, cows, pigs, ponies, and poultry. Several rare breeds are part of this collection, like the Herdwick black-faced sheep and the Bronze turkeys, so called for the tint on their blackish feathers.

Other tourist attractions in the forest include Barkham Manor Vineyard, site of the Piltdown Man discovery; St. George's Vineyard, with an English wine exhibition; the Bluebell Railway, a short-run vintage steam train; Sheffield Park Garden, one hundred flowering acres with an arboretum and two lakes; and Wilderness Wood, advertised as "a family-run Wealden Woodland."

Wilderness Wood sounded closest to the spirit of Pooh. Stopping there late in the afternoon, James and I walked through a deserted yard filled with wooden picnic tables, birdhouses, lattices, and other wood artifacts for sale, into a barn that had been converted into a disarmingly homemade museum. The family who owns the sixty-one acres of Wilderness Wood tends traditional chestnut coppices and plantations of pine, beech, and fir; this particular woodland, a notice proudly claimed, has been providing wood for perhaps a thousand years.

Display boards illustrated the evolution of a natural woodland, the process of coppicing (repeated cutting), and the economics of a working wood. Wilderness Wood clearly aimed at educational groups as well as drop-in visitors. Stretched rather disconcertingly on one board was the skin of a badger, killed on the main road. (BADGERS FEED IN THE WOOD ON WORMS, BEETLES, NUTS, SEEDS, AND ROOTS.) Next to the board on a shelf was the badger's small sharp skull. (PLEASE HANDLE VERY CAREFULLY.)

Since rain was now falling heavily, we decided not to investigate the tree-identification trail or the longer walks on the property. On our way home I kept seeing signs of other promising walks, sheltered parking areas with picnic tables, and roads leading into unknown territory. Ashdown Forest, we agreed, would take more than another trip to explore.

In *The Enchanted Places*, Christopher Milne remembers his childhood excursions to the Forest: "Only those who could walk to the Forest went there. This meant that when we got there we had the Forest almost entirely to ourselves. And this, in turn, made us feel that it was *our* Forest and so made it possible for an imaginary world—Pooh's world—to be born within the real world." The real world of Ashdown Forest, and the imaginary one, happily, are still there.

A FEW FLOATING FACTS

Remember to omit the prefix "0" from an English telephone number when calling from the United States.

For suggestions on where to stay, see "A Few Floating Facts" at the end of Chapter Twenty, "Bluebell Woods."

Rereading the Pooh stories will prepare you for the landscape you'll see: Shepard's drawings are uncannily accurate. At the beginning of *The Enchanted Places*, Christopher Milne supplies a map of the main Pooh sites, such as Owl's House, Six Pine Trees, and the North Pole. He reports: "Anybody who has read the stories knows the Forest and doesn't need me to describe it. Pooh's Forest and Ashdown Forest are identical."

Ann Thwaite's biography, *A. A. Milne* (1990), a full, fluent, and engrossing study of a complex man and writer, will further enrich your travels in Pooh country.

The Forest Centre, Wych Cross, Forest Row, East Sussex RH18 5JP, telephone 01342-823583, is open from two to five during the week, eleven to five weekends, all year.

15

Lord of the Manor: Staying at Standen

It need not cost a lord's ransom to stay for a week in a grand country house. Even if you live in converted servants' quarters, as at Standen, you can still pretend that the whole house and grounds are yours.

It is not easy to recline with aplomb in one's bath while receiving strangers, but James carried it off very well. We had arrived an hour before for a week's stay at Standen, a Victorian country house owned by the National Trust near East Grinstead. As we drove toward the house, we noticed a large tent pitched on the lawn. Although Standen was officially closed for the day, dozens of cars were parked along the drive, and women in silk dresses, accompanied by men in dark suits and discreet ties, were strolling toward the tent.

As she showed us around our second-floor holiday flat, Gladys, one of Standen's resident staff, told us tonight was the annual Lord Mayor's reception. It was obviously quite a to-do. While we lugged suitcases and groceries from the car, we caught glimpses of several men in satin vests, gilt braid, and scarlet sashes, the kind of gaudy ceremonial regalia that

Americans tend to associate either with light opera or the British Empire.

While I unpacked, James ran a bath. The tub in the large old-fashioned bathroom was the original mammoth Victorian fixture, enclosed in a heavily varnished oak casing. To climb in, one first stepped on an attached wooden platform. James loves baths, and, tossing in some of my scented foaming oil, he ran this one almost to the edge of the tub. Sinking into the hot water, he was in bliss.

From the tub, James could look toward a window above the gardens. When I brought in the soap, I glanced out and noticed several partygoers pacing among the roses and cat-mint. Still unpacking, I thought no more about the gala until I was startled by a frantic knocking. I hurried to our front door and opened it. Standing there was a worried-looking man in an official National Trust jacket. I remembered seeing him talking to Gladys when we came in. But we clearly had no time for proper introductions. He was quite agitated and spoke quickly as he stepped inside. As he turned and hurried down the hall, I caught only a few phrases: "Terribly sorry . . . hate to disturb . . . have you noticed a problem with the WC?"

"Uh, actually, my husband is in there right now, in the bath," I called out, and our visitor slowed just a little as he reached the bathroom door. I relented. This was evidently an emergency. "But go on in, I'm sure it's all right," I added, following him to the door and opening it. "James?" I called. "Someone here to check the toilet."

As I stood at the door, the National Trust official almost ran across the floor and looked out the window. He barely glanced at James, who was stretched out in the tub, only ephemerally covered by bubbles. Our visitor flushed the toilet, put down its varnished seat, climbed on it, and peered out the window once more. From my vantage point, the composed scene was striking: the oak-cased tub with James lolling inside, a broad rear view of the National Trust kneeling on the Victorian toilet, and a bit of flowering gardens beyond. James splashed, a little tentatively; our guest, muttering apologetically, flushed again.

Then, climbing down from his perch, he suddenly seemed to realize where he was. Still apologizing, he studiously averted his eyes and virtually sidestepped out of the bathroom. "Goodbye," James said pleasantly, splashing again.

I closed the bathroom door and walked with our guest down the hall. "Water coming down the wall . . . thought it was the cistern . . . overflow . . . so sorry," he said, and left almost as hurriedly as he'd come.

After dinner that night, while the lawn party was gathered in the tent, James and I walked in the garden. Underneath our bathroom window was a pipe that opened directly onto the path below. We saw what had happened. James had filled the tub too full, the overflow valve had emptied into the pipe, and water had begun cascading onto the path—in full view of the distinguished guests wandering through the garden. No wonder our National Trust representative was worried if he'd thought it was the toilet.

Not long afterward, we got ready for bed and turned out the lights. We heard cars crunching on gravel as the party broke up. Just as I was dropping off to sleep, our doorbell rang. We both sat up as if we'd been shot. Who could be wanting us at this hour of night? Tucking in his worn red plaid pajamas, James got up and hustled down two flights to the outside door. When he returned a short time later, he was grinning.

"This is my night for entertaining," he said. "That was someone from the Lord Mayor's party. He'd left his street clothes in the main house and didn't know how else to get them. Our door leads into the corridor, you know."

"What did he say about your pajamas?" I asked curiously.

"Oh, nothing. Far too polite," James answered, getting back into bed.

As I drifted into sleep, I thought that our first night at Standen, a stately country house, had been deliciously appropriate. James had had a chance to practice the art of the levée, albeit in his bath rather than in his bed. And an attendant of the Lord Mayor had paid us a call, a fitting gesture toward those (us) who were (for a week) residents of the local showpiece.

On our way to Gatwick the year before, we'd stopped at nearby Standen on a moment's whim. It is nestled into a steep slope above the Medway Valley, where in the distance a shining reservoir lies between heavily wooded hills. Designed in the 1890s by Philip Webb, a friend and colleague of William Morris's, Standen is filled with understated ornamentation as well as Morris furnishings, wallpaper, and textiles.

Although Standen's official guidebook deprecatingly suggests that its gardens are rather a hodge-podge, with "more to offer the plantsman than those interested in garden-design," they are varied and exuberant. Grassy paths wind in and around a formal enclosed garden, while other gravel paths lead past flowering borders to the upper lawns and then high above the house to a long terrace. On our first visit, we discovered a croquet pitch as smooth as a bowling green enclosed by towering massed rhododendrons, a wildflower meadow, and many paths we did not have time to explore.

"What a marvelous place this would be to live," I sighed as we were getting ready to leave. Stopping to browse in the National Trust shop, I noticed a brochure that listed the many holiday flats the Trust offers for weekly rental. Two, I saw, were available at Standen in what was once a service wing of the house. A year later we were back—this time to live, if only for a week.

As our first evening at Standen had promised, our stay there was full of unanticipated pleasures. Mornings we had breakfast in the spacious sitting room, where we could lounge over coffee brewed in our own kitchen and look out at the early mists floating over the valley. Since the house and garden did not open until afternoon, we were free to walk the grounds for hours as if the property were ours.

One walk led across stiles and through pastures to the far reservoir. Another turned down into a dense woods, across picturesque bridges and through deep dells. Still another, close to the house, dipped suddenly into a disused little stone quarry, now turned into a dense fernery. At the bottom, almost overgrown and hidden from the world above, a small fountain played quiet and melancholy music.

As residents of the holiday flat, we were allowed to tour the main house during its open hours as often as we wished. Soon the ticket takers knew us by sight, and we ambled casually inside with a proprietorial air I hoped the other tourists noticed. I learned to know Standen, not quite as an insider, but as a familiar friend, in a way I never had experienced an English country house before.

In the morning room, a small, sunny, and cozy retreat meant to be used mostly by the women of the house, I could imagine myself retiring for a few quiet hours after breakfast.

If I lived here, I would sink blissfully into a comfy-looking Morris armchair, I thought, and then ask for mid-morning tea to be set down on the polished mahogany table designed by Webb. I would sip tea and munch on a few scones while relishing sunshine (at least occasionally) and views. Facing east into the morning light, the morning room windows opened onto the same panorama of valley, water, and woods that we enjoyed in our holiday flat.

After tea I might read, I decided, as I studied the bookcase, filled with genteel leather-bound volumes that lined one wall, or I might just sit by the window and delight in the sparkle of light on the wet green lawns. If I looked up from my book, I could let my gaze linger on the glowing green, gold, blue, and deep red of the turn-of-the-century ceramics, large plates and vases, set off by white shelves and dark wood tables. Or I could lose myself in the intricate swirls and scrolls of Morris patterns, chintz wall-hangings, cushions, and upholstery.

When I walked through the conservatory, I always wanted to stretch out in one of the cane steamer chairs. Light poured in here, too, not only from above, through the glass roof whose cast-iron frame looked surprisingly airy and delicate, but also from floor-to-ceiling windows that looked out on a pebbled terrace and the upper gardens. A floor of soft red tiles provided an earth-tone background for luxuriant potted palms, fragrant jasmine, and blue-flowered plumbago. (My brochure told me the ever-vigilant architect Webb had decided these unglazed tiles would be "more comfortable to walk on in hobnailed country boots." My own faded athletic shoes felt at that moment quite inappropriate.)

Standen was designed with twelve bedrooms on its second (British first) floor, nine more on the floor above. Of the few open to visitors, I imagined choosing for myself Larkspur, a room named for Morris's wallpaper of swirling foliage on a muted green background. I loved its simple but extraordinarily handsome arts and crafts furniture: polished dark mahogany chests and tables with silver handles, as well as a rush-seated armchair designed by the poet and painter Dante Gabriel Rossetti for Morris & Co. I could read Rossetti from a slim leather-bound volume, sitting in his personally designed chair, before washing up in my spacious dressing room next door, and then turn back a fastidious cut-lace white bedspread on my gleaming brass bed.

With leisurely, repeated visits, I had time—so seldom available in once-through tours of grand houses—to notice and savor details. In the drawing room, I eventually focused on an original light-fitting, a large sconce of hammered copper with decorative sunflower relief, from which hung a fluted glass shade. It was unostentatiously unique, a small work of art Webb had envisioned as part of his grand scheme.

Throughout the house I also paid appreciative attention to the many ingenious *fitted* (built-in) shelves, cupboards, dressers, and wardrobes, all designed by Webb himself, and I soon understood why Standen would have been both a convenient and comfortable place to live.

James also kept noting new architectural details. We now have a collection of snapshots of Standen's many white-painted deal fireplaces, each with a subtly different design. (These fireplaces will probably reappear someday, transmuted, in one of his own houses.) As he walked through the rooms again and again, he, too, made Standen his own.

Although we left Standen part of every day to explore the surrounding countryside, we always looked forward to our return in late afternoon. After supper we descended the spiraling stairs from our flat and opened a private back door into the gardens. Stopping frequently to examine unusual or fragrant flowers, we circled the roses, perennial beds, orchard, rhododendron dell, and bamboo garden at a slow and stately pace, as if I were wearing long skirts and carrying a parasol.

Then we strolled along the gravel paths, turning this way and then that, until we finally climbed to the upper terrace. We sat briefly on each one of many benches thoughtfully placed at different perspectives along the path. Our last stop was always the summerhouse, a small brick gazebo, open on one side but sheltered from rain and wind. Here we could sit in isolated splendor, looking over the tranquil valley, past the lake that was Weirwood Reservoir, into the blurred green shapes of Ashdown Forest many miles away. Sometimes we waited until dusk had shaded into darkness, covering the gardens below, before we returned to the house.

One night, alerted by Standen's curator, we waited until darkness was complete and then walked very quietly to the corner of Hollybush farmhouse, the fifteenth-century tile-hung building that adjoins Standen. The curator had told us that the residents of Hollybush put food out every night for a family of badgers who lived in the woodland across the road. Just when we could barely glimpse anything at all in the unlit darkness, we saw a large, lumbering form emerge from the hedge by the road. It saw us, too, and retreated. Not wanting to disturb the badger, we quickly returned to our flat. But we felt, as temporary proprietors, we had been given a special glimpse of Standen's wildlife.

Our week at Standen passed so quickly, I could not even notice any fading in the riotously thick purple catmint or any fallen petals from white shrub roses in the garden. The night before we had to leave, James and I walked as usual to the summerhouse. It was a clear summer evening, and the birds were still calling gently through the twilight. We sat for a long while, trying to fix in our minds the view and the now-familiar outline of Standen itself. After a long while James said reluctantly, "I suppose we should go in. It's probably time for a bath and bed. We'll have to be up quite early in the morning."

As we walked back to the house, I remembered bath and bed on our first night at Standen. In a week we had gone from high excitement to deep tranquillity. We had, in fact, settled in. If the Lord Mayor came to call tonight, I thought, we'd be quite ready to receive him.

A FEW FLOATING FACTS

Remember to omit the prefix "0" from an English telephone number when calling from the United States. Prices are calculated at $1.60 to the pound.

Standen House has two holiday flats: the larger has three bedrooms and sleeps five, and the smaller has two bedrooms and sleeps three. Both are available between March and December. In 1995, prices per week ranged (according to season and size of flat) from £226 ($361) to £625 ($1000).

To reserve a week or more at Standen, call the National Trust Holiday Booking Office at 01225-791199, or fax your request to 01225-706209. You can charge your booking by credit card.

For further details about renting cottages and flats, not only from the National Trust but other sources, see Chapter One, "How to Be Your Own Travel Agent."

Directions on how to reach Standen, and on its hours of opening, can be found at the end of Chapter Twenty.

16

Lynmouth: Savoring an English Honey Pot

At dusk, I like to walk from our rented cottage down to Lynmouth's tiny harbor. "Beware the twin honey pots of Lynton and Lynmouth," an English guidebook once warned me, before my first visit to these two small towns (combined population, 2100) in Exmoor on the North Devon coast. I am intrigued by caveats, however, and once I saw Lynmouth, whose whitewashed and half-timbered cottages cluster at the foot of high hogback cliffs, I knew I would return again and again.

In high season, both Lynmouth and Lynton, a slightly larger town spread out on the plateau above, are full of vacationers who seek out the surrounding hills, moors, and deep valleys of what has been called England's Little Switzerland. Tourism is, in fact, the only significant local industry. But in early summer or fall, the honey pots, sweeter than ever, do not attract so many buzzing tourists.

Both in early June and in September, James and I have settled happily for a week in a rented cottage in Lynmouth, where, in addition to the pleasures of the village itself, we have found we can enjoy all kinds of walking excursions, both short jaunts and longer hikes.

As the sun turns the seaside cliffs into shades of red and purple, I often leave our fenced hillside garden, with its apple tree and rosebushes, and pass through a vine-covered gate into a narrow paved path that winds abruptly down past bed-and-breakfasts. Emerging into Lynmouth Street, a block-long pedestrian shopper's precinct, I wonder how anyone could find this town's tourist offerings tawdry. I like the seaside air of the little shops, whose windows and outdoor baskets display multicolored sticks of candy, seashells, leather wallets, boxes of fudge, bottles of *scrumpy* (local high-wattage cider), and racks of postcards and maps.

At the end of the street, an ice cream kiosk plastered with tempting colored pictures sells morello cherry, tutti-frutti, apricot, chocolate toffee—all topped with clotted Devon cream. Clotted cream on ice cream: the thought alone can stop one's arteries cold, but what glorious superfluity!

One early June night, a string of colored lights outlined the bay window of a café on Lynmouth Street, where two couples, talking and laughing, were having dinner. They sat unselfconsciously in the window, just inches from the street. As I strolled by, I felt as if they set the tone for the evening, one of intimate enjoyment in a modest vacation town that does not make too much of a fuss over its visitors.

Dusk was deepening when I reached the end of the long stone pier that juts out from the town's main street. Standing alone on the pier, the tide out, I watched the small fishing fleet—just four boats that June night—motor into the harbor. The harbor was already filled with gaily painted pleasurecraft and sailboats. No luxury yachts: fancy folk don't come to Lynmouth.

Looking back at Lynmouth, I could see lights from the few shop windows along the waterfront gleam into the harbor.

The illuminated Tors Hotel, grandly set two hundred feet above the sea on Countisbury Hill, looked like a multifaceted jewel in the increasing darkness. The Rising Sun, an ancient inn that climbs Mars Hill behind the pier, shone its welcoming lights along the town's main street.

Three or four customers drifted in and out of Aladdin's Cave, a souvenir shop in an octagonal Victorian tower, and a few more hovered around a fish-and-chips shop next door. I could see that the bright red public phone booth was occupied, with one person waiting outside. Nothing in Lynmouth looked deserted, but nothing was crowded.

A soft breeze blew in from the sea. Sometimes the wind is fierce and the seas high, but that night the weather was unusually gentle. Two fishermen arrived at the end of the pier with their long poles, evidently planning to settle in for several hours. With still some rose-colored light left, I decided to walk along the sea in a different direction.

My route took me over a bridge to the public Manor Grounds, a well-clipped grassy area with playground equipment, a putting green, and tennis courts, all maintained by the Lynmouth/Lynton Town Council. A path led from there to the rocky beach under the cliffs. As I walked along the paved path, I noticed some of the civilized subtleties that make some small English towns seem so attuned to basic human needs.

Behind the Manor Grounds stood a large handsome white building with several wings, its many multipaned windows looking out toward the sea. It was a residence for the elderly, and a few gray-haired and stooped people were still out that evening on the putting green. The residence reminded me of Lynton's Cottage Hospital high above, an informal rambling building that looked disarmingly comfortable.

At the end of the path, I passed a low stone shelter with a glassed enclosure containing benches so townspeople and visitors can sit and enjoy a view of the sea during inclement weather. Beyond the path, two signs reminded me how Lynmouth is still an integral part of the wild and beautiful landscape of Exmoor. WARNING: SILLERY STEPS WASHED AWAY, BEWARE OF INCOMING TIDE says one placard; the other points walkers toward the Devon Coastal Path—7 MILES TO COUNTY GATE, 10 MILES TO CULBONE, 20 TO MINEHEAD.

Scrambling over the pebbly beach, I skirted huge boulders, looking like a giant's playthings, tumbled down from the cliffs toward the edge of the shore. They were carelessly heaped together as if the giant had been told to hurry and put them away before coming in to dinner. I picked my way cautiously down to the water's edge and tested it with my hand. It was surprisingly warm. Behind me, Lynmouth's lights twinkled as if it were a toy town at Christmas.

If dusk and evenings in Lynmouth inspire quiet and meditative moods, days can be quite lively. Lynmouth is the hub for a number of memorable walks. One begins above, in Lynton, and to reach it I buy a ticket on the Cliff Railway, a nearly vertical track of 862 feet running from Lynmouth's waterfront up to the center of Lynton. James, braver than I am in all else, prefers to walk the zigzag path to the top.

The Cliff Railway, opened in 1890, is ingenious. Two small tramcars are linked together by two steel cables. Each car has a 700-gallon water tank which is filled at the top and emptied at the bottom, causing the lower car to be pulled up to Lynton while the heavier car from the top descends to Lynmouth. It creaks and groans, while the passengers on its almost perpendicular slant get exhilarating—and terrifying—views of the sea below and beyond. The trip takes less than ten minutes, but it seems longer.

At the top of the railway, a turn to the right leads to the North Walk, a wide paved pathway cut high into the cliffs above the sea. At first the North Walk passes a few Lynton hotels, jammed precariously into the near-vertical hillside, but a hiker is soon surrounded only by land, water, and sky. For more than a mile, it is possible to walk in silence, listening to sea birds and waves far beneath.

Wild goats sometimes strike dramatic poses on rocky outcroppings below the path. A few local residents may be out for a stroll with their dogs, and of course an occasional tourist wanders by, but the North Walk is often almost deserted. At dusk and later, on clear nights, the lights of Wales signal across the Bristol Channel, and winking steamers slip in and out of the darkness.

Because we love the North Walk so much, with its sense of seclusion and its immensity of sea and sky, James and I seldom give deserving attention to what lies at the far end of the walk. The Valley of the Rocks is one of Lynton's most-advertised attractions, a strange and haunting valley with weird rock formations, suitably named Ragged Jack, the Devil's Cheesewring, and the White Lady. A road from Lynton leads to a parking lot in the deep valley, though taking the North Walk or another waymarked path across Hollerday Hill can successfully avoid any traffic. Early in the morning or at evening, few tourists are clambering over these rocks, and we easily escape them by walking farther on the South West Peninsula Coastal Path, out of sight of cars and people, far enough to look back and admire the jagged profile of the valley.

For truly hardy walkers, the Coastal Path continues on,

eventually circling past four bays to the west. One sheltered
bay, Heddon's Mouth, is also a short though painstakingly
slow drive from Lynmouth, five miles west along a narrow,
winding coastal road. Just beyond the village of Martinhoe, at
a much-frequented watering hole called Hunter's Inn, a footpath begins that follows the rift cut by the River Heddon to
the sea. The walk is an easy mile and a half through a beautiful woodland valley, and on sunny days the path is dotted
with amiable tourists, often British families, with women in
bright sundresses, open-backed clogs, and high heels—not the
serious high-booted ramblers one encounters on the Coastal
Path.

My favorite walking country near Lynmouth is on Brendon
Common. About fifteen minutes from Lynmouth in the heart
of Exmoor, Brendon Common is an open moorland with the
Bristol Channel on one distant horizon. In moments after
parking in one of several waysides, a walker is out of sight or
sound of the road, alone with purple heather, golden gorse,
streams, birds, wild ponies, red deer, and a cloud-hung sky
that seems to encompass and float over everything.

Many paths cut across the hills, some signposted to Doone
Country, a valley identified with R. D. Blackmore's classic
novel, and others to villages like Malmsmead or Brendon.
One can walk in the clear, sharp air for an hour, or three, or
six, and never retrace one's steps. There is all the space to
breathe I could ever want on Brendon Common.

To find wonderful walks, however, it is not necessary to
drive outside of Lynmouth. The Glen Lyn Estate in the middle of town includes a spectacular narrow gorge down which
the West Lyn River tumbles and foams over rocky shelves.
The gorge is open to visitors, who can scramble alongside it on

a fern-bordered path that leads up, up, and up. The noise of the falling river is so fierce that it cuts off conversation, and although the shallow water does not look particularly dangerous, it is. Following heavy rains on water-soaked Exmoor in 1952, a disastrous flood swept through Lynmouth, taking houses, cars, and thirty-four people with it. The Flood Memorial Hall provides a sobering reminder of that night.

The Memorial Hall also stands on the site of the old lifeboat station, where a celebrated rescue was carried out in 1899. During a raging storm, the station staged an overland launch that involved dragging the heavy lifeboat up Countisbury Hill, a precipitous slope with a 1:4 gradient, across the cliffs and down to Porlock Harbor. Driving down Countisbury Hill today, one notices several *escape roads*, nearly vertical turnoffs banked in sand, where an out-of-control automobile can presumably turn away from disaster. It is almost impossible to imagine the teams of horses and straining men pulling the lifeboat up this awesome hill.

Another walk from the center of Lynmouth follows the East Lyn River to Watersmeet, designated a National Trust "beauty spot," where Hoar Oak Water joins the East Lyn. This twisting path is virtually a tunnel of green on the hillside, thickly overhung with trees and shrubs, with fern-covered banks below. The East Lyn ripples over its stone-strewn bed with a low murmur, a lulling sound just as deceptive as the gaily splashing gorge of the West Lyn. Here, too, in 1952, the waters rose with destructive fury.

But on a bright day in Lynmouth, when visitors lounge in deck chairs along Riverside Road or browse in the cheerful shops along Lynmouth Street, or at dusk, when fishing boats glide into the harbor, the town seems far removed from the dramatic events of its past. It welcomes visitors quietly, and it promises them an unhurried pace of seaside and river walks, moorland explorations, and leisurely strolls through the town itself.

Lynmouth is also a center for many Exmoor excursions, all within an hour's drive: great country houses like Arlington Court, gardens like Marwood Hill near Barnstaple, Dunster Castle, tiny Culbone Church, the almost-too-picturesque village of Selworthy Green, Cleeve Abbey, the bustling seaside resort of Minehead. But for those who are content with a little honey pot whose gentle but pungent flavors linger a long while afterward, Lynmouth itself is quite enough.

A FEW FLOATING FACTS

Remember to omit the prefix "0" from an English telephone number when calling from the United States. Prices are calculated at $1.60 to the pound.

We rented our cottage, Lyndale House, from Mrs. E. Oxenham, Glen Lyn Cottage, Lynmouth, N. Devon, EX35 6ER, telephone Lynton 01598-753207. She has several such properties in Lynmouth. Price for each property according to season and number of guests, from £140 ($224) per week to £395 ($632) per week. Available April to September.

Other attractive possibilities: The Tors Hotel, set high above Lynmouth on Countisbury Hill, has magnificent views and a heated outdoor pool. Bed and breakfast from £35 ($56) to £52 ($83.20) per person for a double room with breakfast, from

£35 ($56) to £85 ($136) for a single room. Telephone 01598-753236, fax 01598-752544.

The picturesque and much-photographed Rising Sun Inn, a fourteenth-century inn with thatched roof, sits at the end of the quay in Lynmouth, telephone 01598-753223, fax 01598-753480. Some private baths. From about £40 ($64) per person for bed and breakfast.

Shelley's Cottage, a charming, thatched-roof cottage with a four-poster bed and private garden, so named because the poet Shelley spent his honeymoon there in 1812, is £59 ($92) per person for bed and breakfast.

The Bath Hotel, Harbourside, Lynmouth, telephone 01598-752280 or -752238, fax 01598-752544 (same as Tors Hotel), is in the center of the village, a few steps from the harbor. The hotel has its own salmon weir, providing in season the only fresh salmon available locally. Bed and breakfast from £27 ($43) to £37 ($59) per person.

Several hotels with superb views line the North Walk between Lynton and Lynmouth. They have a Lynton address. A helpful listing of hotels, bed-and-breakfast accommodations, rental cottages, and holiday flats (fully equipped) in the Lynmouth and Lynton area can be obtained from Lyn Publicity Association, Town Hall, Lee Road, Lynton, N. Devon. An Exmoor National Park Information Centre is located on the Esplanade in Lynmouth. Walking maps of the area are sold at both.

17

Two Scottish War Memorials

*Any traveler who follows the thumbprint school—slowing down
and stopping for at least a week in one spot—finds that he or she
has time for small events that often turn out to be not so small after
all. Their reverberations can set the tone of a entire trip.*

*Although these two war memorials are very special places, an
alert reader will immediately notice the fact that they are in Scotland—not in England, properly speaking. What, then, are they
doing in a book about England? See the note just before Chapter
Eleven, "Gentle Walks in the Wild Highlands," for what I hope is
a convincing explanation.*

T he war is not over in Scotland. All through Great Britain, any alert visitor notices well-tended monuments
to the dead of World Wars I and II—stained-glass
windows in country churches, obelisks in town squares, and
plaques in public buildings. The grass is cut around these monuments, fresh flowers are placed below the windows, and the
brass is regularly polished. Sometimes the names of those who
died between 1939 and 1945 are appended to the much longer
list from 1914 to 1919. The World War appears continuous.

But in Scotland, memory is even fresher and rawer. Here

they mourn not only the twentieth-century wars but the long, bitter, and intermittently violent struggle with England that effectively ended with the defeat of Bonnie Prince Charlie at Culloden in 1746. Entwined with this struggle are brutal sagas of clan warfare, such as the famous Glencoe Massacre of 1692, when a militia of Campbells, urged on by the English, rose one February dawn against their Highland hosts, MacIain's MacDonalds, and turned the dark, mountainous pass into the Glen of Weeping.

Under mist-filled gray skies, the spectacularly bleak Highland landscape itself sometimes seems to be in mourning. Relentless logging, followed by overgrazing from sheep and deer, eventually transformed the old Caledonian forests into barren, rocky slopes; infertile, heather-dotted moorland; and acid peat bogs. During the 1800s, the infamous *clearances*, forcing Highland tenants off the land to make room for sheep pastures, emptied most of the northern glens. Heaps of tumbledown stones mark now-deserted *clearance villages*.

In such an atmosphere, war memorials seem strikingly current, inescapable reminders of the devastation created by man, even in this remote and beautiful part of the world. One September, during three weeks in the Highlands, James and I visited two very different such memorials.

On a bright Sunday afternoon we walked out the door of the Culloden Visitor Centre, not far from Inverness, and were uncannily transported to April 16, 1746. We had joined a special tour given by the White Cockade Society, named after the defiant badge of Prince Charlie's followers. In full period costume, the members of the society took the parts of various actual participants in the massacre.

Our guide, dressed in a scarlet and blue officer's uniform

complete with gilt-edged tricorne and sword, led us around
Drumossie Moor, where the battle took place. At each stop he
interviewed one of the amateur actors, perhaps a confident
British soldier, or a fiercely Jacobite member of the Irish
Brigade, or a grimly defiant Highlander, or a Highlander's
hysterically sobbing wife. Their stories, threaded together
with a continued narrative from our guide, effectively turned
the sunny heather-covered moor, bordered by a well-used
modern highway, into the wind-swept, sleet-drenched, boggy
wasteland of 1746.

Flags marked the opposing battle lines. Signs noted where
each clan or regiment had stood or fallen. Our guide pointed
out where the clansmen's advance had failed, where certain
chiefs were slaughtered, where other Highlanders had huddled in their tartans against the cold as they awaited word of
what they already knew was a doomed attack.

At the hour's end, we paused at the Well of the Dead,
where defeated and dying clansmen had crawled for a drink
of water, only to be cut down by the victorious pursuing English. Our guide told us of other atrocities. I thought of Bosnia,
Somalia, Iraq, Cambodia, a roll call that seemed endless.

As we concluded the tour, our guide informed us that this
one hour had coincided with the actual length of the battle.
"While we have been walking around the moor, the two sides
engaged and Prince Charlie's forces have been defeated. It is
all over now," he said, gesturing at the flags still flying on the
moor. But despite the warm sunshine, the glow of purple
heather in bloom, and the peaceful hills in a blue distance, I
did not feel that it was over at all.

After we had visited Culloden, I kept thinking of our very
first afternoon in the Highlands. On that earlier Sunday,

James and I wanted to explore for a few hours near our rented cottage outside Gairloch, a small village on the northwest coast. From a guidebook of local walks, we chose one that began only a half mile from our front door.

As we began the walk, leaving the road to follow a stony cart track into the hills, I read to James about our destination. There, at an inland glacial lake called a Fairy Loch, a U.S.A.A.F. B-24H Liberator had crashed on June 13, 1945. Carrying a crew of nine and six Air Force passengers home after the war, the aircraft had left Glasgow for the long trip to America. Somehow its pilot had lost his way, or perhaps the engine had failed.

According to eyewitnesses, the plane emerged from thick cloud just beyond Loch Gairloch. It struck the top of Slioch, the tallest mountain in the area, and lost some bomb bay door ports. Then, probably looking for a place to ditch, the plane circled over Loch Gairloch. On the run in, as the guidebook said with a painful obliqueness, "they just failed to clear the rocky spurs by the Fairy Lochs." All aboard were killed.

Our rough track soon carried us out of sight of the road. Before long we began to climb steadily through a birch woodland and then emerged onto open moor. Like our day at Culloden, the weather was uncharacteristically bright and sunny. The moor shimmered with purple heather, and in especially wet and boggy places, grasses grew thickly in a deceptively inviting green. But it was still hard not to feel subdued. The low rocky hills, bare of trees, were overshadowed by fantastically eroded mountains on the horizon. Nowhere could I see any sign of human life.

After an hour, the cart track descended to Loch Braigh Horrisdale, a still expanse of gray water that lapped around a boggy, heather-strewn shore. Here we followed our guide-book's directions and turned onto what it called "an indistinct path." In fact, as we quickly began to sink into the boggy up-land, we often could not see a path at all. Struggling across several small rocky slopes, with an ominous squishing sound to each step, we saw a cairn on the far side of a wide, flat marshland. That was the entrance to the hidden Fairy Loch.

Already my shoes were wet, my footing uneasy, and my spirits somewhat shaken. Several times my walking stick had saved me from plunging deeper into the sucking bog than I cared to think about. But we had gone too far to turn back. I had also begun to believe we were on some kind of strange pil-grimage. We were evidently bound to seek the American Lib-erator, and this disappearing, marshy path was one of the necessary obstacles.

Over a last rise, we suddenly found ourselves looking down on the Fairy Loch. It was a small, secret lake, what the Scots call a *lochan*, whose banks rose up to rocky walls. At first, as we cautiously descended to the lake and began to walk around its perimeter, I did not see anything unusual. Then the sun, shining on the still water, caught a flashing gleam of metal. There, rising from the shallow lake like a sword, was the sleek silver blade of a propeller.

Something about that propeller made me catch my breath. It looked so incongruous, thrusting out of the water, and yet, oddly, it also seemed to belong there. The ancient standing stones scattered throughout Scotland often cast that kind of spell. As we walked closer, we began to notice other bits of wreckage: what may have been part of the plane's undercar-riage, half covered by heather on a tiny island in the middle of the lake; jagged pieces of metal among the tufts of bog grass.

At the head of the loch, we stopped for a long while before a brass plate embedded in the rock face of the high crag that had caught the plane and brought it down. The plate had been given, its inscription said, by friends and family of those who had died there. It named the passengers and crew of the Liberator, adding their ranks, ages, and hometowns. Almost none had been over twenty-three years old.

Nearly fifty years had passed, but the crash felt as if it might have happened yesterday. The shining bits of metal, the displaced propeller, the somber list of the dead, all gave us the sense of having intruded upon a disaster. The only fitting response was to stand in silence for a time and grieve.

When we slowly began our return journey, picking our way across more bogland, James and I talked in unusually quiet tones about what we had seen. At nineteen, James had served in World War II in England and then Belgium. He might have been on that Liberator, he said. I flinched, thinking not only of him and myself, but of those other wives, other families, all those irrevocably changed lives. And the young men themselves, so achingly young, what of them? They had thought their war was over; they were going home. Who knows what they felt as they emerged from the clouds over Loch Gairloch? As they headed downward on that final, fatal approach?

"I am glad they have left the site as it was," James said. I nodded. These American soldiers had fought in Europe and died in Scotland, but their memorial was universal. Yet it was also fittingly Scottish, imbued with the sense of history still alive—and of tragedy that never seemed to end. Anyone who circled Drumossie Moor, or who confronted the shining propeller in the Fairy Loch, would have to admit that the war wasn't over.

18

Secret Gardens of the City of London

When visitors to London tour the City, the traditional square mile that was the ancient center of Britain's capital, they expect to see its great commercial and financial institutions, such as the Bank of England, the Stock Exchange, or Lloyds. They inevitably stop at St. Paul's Cathedral and perhaps one or two of Wren's remaining smaller churches. At night they often flock to the Barbican, home of the London Symphony Orchestra and the Royal Shakespeare Company. What they don't usually have an opportunity to see are the City's gardens.

Hidden among new towering office buildings, preserved in small out-of-the-way parks, or quietly flourishing behind unnoticed gates, these gardens range from tiny pockets of greenery to a luxuriant tropical conservatory. James and I discovered these flowering oases one April when, during a week's stay near Smithfield Market, we noticed in our *Good Gardens Guide* a full page of briefly annotated City listings. Neither of us had ever thought of a self-guided garden tour in the commercial heart of London. But even to those who return often, London is full of surprises. Marking several possible routes to connect the green squares on our detailed street map, we set off. Our routes sometimes swerved outside the City's boundaries.

Although a determined walker could probably cover the main City gardens in one long day, we took three half-days. Not only do City streets offer many detours—museums, shops, restaurants—but they are a compendium of contemporary English architecture. Much of the City was destroyed by bombing in World War II, and in recent years rebuilding has transformed the skyline. Since James is a modernist architect, he looked upward, not always approvingly, while I looked downward at our map.

Our first stop was Fortune Street Garden, just outside the City, a modest urban way station surrounded by once-trendy examples of post–World War II housing. The exposed-concrete mass of the Barbican, which includes a housing development for more than six thousand people, loomed on one side, a postmodern building with curves and flourishes on another, a faded Sixties-style apartment building on a third. The small, unpretentious green rectangle below did not seem much garden for all those people. But on an early April morning, though daffodils were blooming and a few roses beginning to bud below the brick walls, Fortune Street Garden was almost deserted. This part of London was obviously the working City, not a place of leisure.

Rain was falling lightly as we tramped through Bunhill Fields, a graveyard between Bunhill Row and City Road. Famous for its tombs and memorials of William Blake, John Bunyan, Daniel Defoe, Isaac Watts, Cromwell's family, and others, Bunhill Fields also had a large well-tended lawn lined with benches and dotted with small beds of flowers. But this garden, too, seemed strangely empty, and—considering the fenced-off graves—rather dismal in the drizzly rain.

So Finsbury Square, only a few blocks farther, was something of a shock. Suddenly, merely by crossing a few busy streets, we were in the heart of a prosperous, spiffed-up City, where the overconfident gleam of the Eighties still lingered. On one side, with its enormous closely clipped lawn, Finsbury Square looked like a giant's putting green. This side was edged by a discreet single-link metal fence and a grassy moat: no sign was needed to keep people off the grass. But the other side, equally a dazzling green, was fenceless and accessible. Between the two sides were benches, a restaurant-bar-brasserie complex with outdoor seating, and an upscale public convenience that was both airy and clean.

If Fortune Street Garden had seemed a little sparse, the plantings here were lavish. Near a bench where we paused, a profusion of primroses in yellow, red, purple, pink, and white spilled over the base of a tree. In other planters and borders, hyacinths, tulips, pansies, and daffodils bloomed with abandon.

On a weekday morning, with business presumably humming in the handsome stone office buildings surrounding the green, an expensive silence pervaded Finsbury Square. Triton Court set the tone. A monumental but graceful Art Deco building refurbished in 1984, Triton Court holds not only twenty-six offices but also an award-winning greenery-filled atrium, the newest kind of City garden.

Admiring this atrium was not easy. A guard snapped to attention when James and I entered the lobby of Triton Court, inquired our intentions, and insisted on locating the manager to authorize my few snapshots. But the glass-roofed atrium itself was inviting, with terraced interior walls hung with trailing greenery and large fig trees clustered around an ornamental pool below. On a cold winter's day, the atrium would feel almost Mediterranean. Taking advantage of this most un-English setting, the Roux brothers, well-known London culinary entrepreneurs, operate several atrium restaurants.

Triton Court's atrium is only one of several such extravagant interior displays in the newly resplendent financial heart of the City. The trees in the inner courtyard at Robert Fleming Holdings Ltd., 25 Copthall Avenue, seemed almost to rise to the glass ceiling. Nearby Lehman Brothers centered its offices around a seven-sided dazzling green marble pool, edged in white marble and encircled by discreet dark gray marble benches. As if watered by money, the ivy was astonishingly thick on the window screens above.

Although most private firms frown on frivolous sightseers (we were admitted, but grudgingly), part of the Broadgate Development in the financial district is accessible to the public. A few shops and a restaurant overlook the Broadgate's amphitheater, a kind of concrete terraced courtyard. Open to the sky and hung with lush greenery, this encircling set of stepped terraces looked rather like a modern-day Hanging Gardens of Babylon.

After this side trip into 1980s opulence, I was relieved to continue on to Finsbury Circus, the largest open space in the City and London's first public park (1606). *Circus* in England usually refers to a busy traffic interchange, crammed with cars and dizzyingly noisy, like Piccadilly Circus, or Oxford Circus. Finsbury Circus, however, was a relic of an earlier and more civilized age. Its stately garden was almost entirely enclosed by dignified low-rise stone buildings, designed as crescents, with mansard roofs and discreet classical ornamentation. Each seemed more quietly regal than the next.

What the occupants of, say, Salisbury House, look out on is a wide expanse of lawn, subdivided by low box hedges, curving pathways, and shrubs. Large areas of bedding plants—in April, tulips, primroses, daffodils—provided color among all this green. Part of the lawn was a bowling green; a further amenity was a small bandstand. In one corner, a whimsical cupola covered a granite drinking fountain, with taps of polished brass, donated in 1902. A few men in dark business suits walked purposefully through the park, but otherwise it was undisturbed.

The tranquillity of Finsbury Circus restored us for a brisk walk to Postman's Park. Located opposite the Main Post Office and National Postal Museum, Postman's Park was a perfect antidote to the excesses of the financial center. A retiring sort of park, its unobtrusive entrance on King Edward Street looked like a gate into a private residential courtyard. We had walked past the gate many times and never realized what a substantial park and garden lay beyond it.

The atmosphere inside the park was subdued, even a little melancholy. An ominous dark statue of a crouching Minotaur, by sculptor Michael Ayrton, brooded in one corner, rather dissipating the cheer of the surrounding flowering shrubs. Even beds of daffodils and tulips could not relieve the somberness of a tiled wall flanking one side of the garden, erected as a Victorian memorial to men, women, and children who had sacrificed themselves for others.

Each tile in the wall recounted a miniature drama. DAVID SELVES, AGED 12, OF WOOLWICH/ SUPPORTED HIS DROWNING PLAYFELLOW AND SANK WITH HIM CLASPED IN HIS ARMS, SEPTEMBER 12, 1886; GEORGE LEE, FIREMAN AT A FIRE IN CLERKENWELL/ CARRIED AN UNCONSCIOUS GIRL TO THE ESCAPE, FALLING SIX

TIMES AND DIED OF HIS INJURIES, JULY 26, 1876; MARY ROGERS, STEWARDESS OF THE STELLA/ SELF-SACRIFICED BY GIVING UP HER LIFE BELT AND VOLUNTARILY GOING DOWN IN THE SINKING SHIP, MARCH 30, 1899. Postman's Park seemed a long, long way from Triton Court.

Life does go on, of course, and so did we. We decided to end our first garden tour with a late lunch at Rudland & Stubbs, an old-fashioned restaurant specializing in fresh fish, just a few minutes walk away in Greenhill's Rents. Men (and a few dressed-for-success women) in City suits filled the small, dark room redolent with such dishes as salmon cakes or a three-fish sampler (John Dory, sole, and bream) on spinach with a spring-onion sauce.

Our second day of daffodil-drenched greenery began at St. Paul's Cathedral. While crowds pushed up the front steps, we turned toward the back of the church. Undiscovered by the tour groups, St. Paul's churchyard was a pleasant meditative garden filled with rosebushes, shrubs, flowers, and benches. Only a few people took advantage of this quiet space on our April morning.

Just across the street, Festival Gardens was also unvisited. Occupying a small city block, this was a sunken garden, mostly lawn, with an edging of flowers. At one end, a fountain poured out water from three bronze lion-head spouts. Above the fountain, a statue of an entwined couple, called *The Young Lovers*, by Georg Ehrlich (1897–1966), tactfully turned its back on the cathedral.

Just down the street, along Cheapside, Cleary Gardens offered still another chance to escape City pavements. Built on several levels, this was an urban garden that made the most of its small space. The walkways and platforms that eventually descended to a bit of green were bedecked with tubs of flowers. Wooden trellises overhead were entwined with roses, and bits of paving tile had been removed for flowering bulbs.

For the rest of the morning we drifted from one delightful garden to another. Some were so small they were almost like a quick green thought between stone and brick buildings, but each had its own charm. Greyfriars, near St. Paul's, on Newgate Street, evocatively combined ruined walls with wooden pillars on which climbing roses had been trained. St. Anne and St. Agnes, on Gresham Street, a corner garden belonging to an existing church, offered several benches backed by raised beds of daffodils and, within even its confined space, a small meandering walk. St. Mary Staining Garden, off Staining Lane, on the site of a vanished church, was a mere tiny green patch, but it boasted a brilliant mixed border of yellow daffodils and red tulips, a flowering magnolia, a bench, and a fresh-looking litter bin. (All the parks we saw were impeccably tidy.)

In Love Lane, St. Mary Aldermanbury Garden was a miniature park filled with flowers, magnolias, and camellias, all set within the low, ruined walls of a Wren church. Small as it was, this garden held much history. The first mention of a church on this site was recorded in 1181, according to a plaque put up by Westminster College of Fulton, Missouri, which had restored the site as a memorial to Winston Churchill. Part of the grounds included a knot garden, adorned with a bust of Shakespeare and dedicated to his fellow actors and friends, John Heminge and Henry Condell, who collected his works. Churchill, Wren, Shakespeare, Heminge and Condell, a twelfth-century church and Fulton, Missouri: we had much to think about under the falling magnolia blossoms.

Also built around the ruins of a Wren church, St. Dunstan's

Church Garden, St. Dunstan's Hill, was perhaps the most enchanting of all these City gardens. It was not a garden anyone
would simply stumble upon. Overshadowed by new office
buildings, the site was down a side street between Lower
Thames Street and Eastcheap, not on a tourist route to anywhere. Because the garden was set on a hill, we climbed steps
to several levels to explore the magical interior.

All but the tower of the Wren church was torn down and
rebuilt again in 1817; then the church was bombed. Some
walls, arches, and Wren's magnificent tower still stand, a romantic backdrop for flowers, shrubs, and creeping vines, as
well as a small fountain and several benches. I asked a young
gardener, hard at work, about plant names. Uncertain himself, he pointed out a regular visitor who, he said, might remember the proper names of some of the sixty-odd shrubs.
The regular, a dapper City man eating his bag lunch by the
fountain, did: daphne, weigela, euphorbia, buddleia, vibur-
num, cistus, passiflora, oakes quirkus roba—I couldn't keep
up. I wondered how many Wall Street bag-lunchers could
have reeled off such a list.

It was lunchtime for us too, and today we had packed our
own picnic. A few minutes away, across Lower Thames Street,
we emerged on Riverside Walkway, on the Thames just outside
the former Billingsgate Market, where fresh fish used to be un-
loaded and sold wholesale. Now, grandly renovated by the
Japanese but never occupied, Billingsgate's enclosed market was
to let. We sat alone on the sunny brick terrace and picnicked
with an unimpeded view of the great river.

After lunch we walked a short distance downriver to a
monumental garden as public and impressive as St. Dunstan's
was quiet and subtle. Trinity Square, just across from the

Tower of London, was the site of an ancient scaffold. Part of it is now occupied by Tower Hill Memorial, dedicated to men of the merchant navy and fishing fleets who died in World War II. Below the scaffold site was a large sunken garden with many shrubs and flowerbeds, and a throng of people moving toward a parking lot and Underground station. But what caught our attention was not the flowers in the garden below but those at our feet.

The scaffold site was marked by a plaque TO COMMEMORATE THE TRAGIC HISTORY AND IN MANY CASES THE MARTYRDOM OF THOSE WHO FOR THE SAKE OF THEIR FAITH, COUNTRY OR IDEALS STAKED THEIR LIVES AND LOST. It included names like Sir Thomas Wyatt, 1554; Sir Thomas More, 1535; Thomas Cromwell, Earl of Essex, 1540; Simon Fraser, Lord Lovat, 1747; and others. Near the plaque lay a plastic sleeve of fresh flowers. I bent down to look more closely.

Stapled to the plastic was a postcard of Thomas Wentworth, first Earl of Strafford, 1593–1641, from the National Portrait Gallery. I turned the card over. On the back, someone had written in pen, BORN GOOD FRIDAY 13 APRIL 1593. DIED 12TH MAY 1641. A GREAT INJUSTICE DONE TO ONE OF OUR GREATEST ENGLISHMEN. IN REMEMBRANCE OF YOUR 400TH BIRTHDAY.

To whom, and why, did Strafford's cruel fate still matter so much after four hundred years? Discussing this anonymous fan of Strafford's, we walked toward home. The last part of our tour led along the London Wall Walk, part of a recent addition to the City, a broad walkway high above the streets. Connecting marble and stone office towers, it runs for many blocks, with outdoor cafés, newsstands, a few shops—its own self-contained world. Wall maps showed us our precise location, and well-marked exits led down to destinations like the

Guildhall or Monument. The walkway offered a superb bird's-eye view of much of the City's newest buildings, as well as several gardens.

From our high perch, we admired St. Alphage Garden, containing bits of the old Roman wall, framed with shrubs, benches, and sunny open spaces. Near the Barbican we descended to stroll on the green lawn of the Barber and Surgeons Hall Gardens, also with bits of the old wall now covered with ivy. The garden belonged to the adjacent new hall, pronounced by James a monstrous postmodern melange of arches, columns, and ornamental doodads. It did make an odd match to the Roman ruin.

Since the Barber and Surgeons Hall Gardens formed part of the corner of a block of Barbican flats, we could also glimpse the vast inner garden and placid pool of the Barbican complex itself. (An even better view can be enjoyed from the terrace of the Barbican Centre, where a café with cheerful awnings over its outdoor tables overlooks the water.)

But we were saving the Barbican for the next day. The *Good Gardens Guide* had informed us of a Barbican Conservatory, open to the public only on weekends and bank holidays, and the next day was Easter Monday. Although we had often attended plays at the Barbican, we had never before realized that it had a private tropical garden.

The Barbican Conservatory was glamorous enough to make one want to move to one of the apartments below, just to be able to visit it every day. Part of the garden was under glass, with gigantic trees growing up to the roof. A huge date palm, for example, weighed two tons when it was planted in 1986. Palm trees, cypress, banyan fig, and others: this was an organized jungle.

Some of the names were as fascinating as the plants: angel's tears, from Brazil, or monstera deliciosa, the Swiss-cheese plant, from Mexico, whose unusual edible fruit, according to its placard, tastes LIKE MIXED FRUIT SALAD. Pondering a Swiss-cheese plant that tasted like fruit salad, I moved from bougainvillea and kafir lilies into the arid garden. There I met another American—"Fred," a saguaro cactus, a gift from Salt Lake City to the City of London.

The conservatory extended to an outdoor terrace, with a rock garden studded with small plants like saxifrage, frittilaria, and allium. Ornamental pools rippled with all kinds of glinting fish, also with intriguing names: ghost koi, golden rudd, lion head, mirror carp, and others. This jewel of a garden even included a tiny octagonal aviary, with birds like the canary, diamond dove, zebra finch, and Peking robin. According to its brochure, the conservatory was now planning a collection of carnivorous plants and an outdoor alpine section.

When we reluctantly left the conservatory, with its rich, fruity aroma of damp soil, heavy foliage, and warm, moist air, we were a little startled to find ourselves on a chilly London street under darkening skies. But as we headed for our flat, we were not dismayed. We would never again think of the City as a gray place of institutions, banks, and offices. We knew it was filled with gardens.

A FEW FLOATING FACTS

Remember to omit the prefix "0" from an English telephone number when calling from the United States.

The City officially claims about 162 open spaces as gardens, though some may be as small as a tree with a bench. The outdoor public gardens of the City are free and easily accessible. A detailed London street map is essential to locate some of them.

Most City gardens are open eight A.M. to seven P.M. or dusk, seven days a week. Postman's Park is open Monday to Friday, seven A.M. to dusk, closed weekends and bank holidays. Bunhill Fields Graveyard Garden is open Monday to Friday, seven-thirty A.M. to seven P.M., four P.M. October to March. St. Paul's Churchyard is open six A.M. to seven-thirty P.M., seven days a week. A few small gardens, without gates, like St. Agnes and St. Anne, St. Mary Aldermanbury, St. Alphage, are open permanently. (All of these times are, of course, subject to change.)

Since our visit, the Barbican Conservatory has decided to open more frequently to the public. For current hours and admission charges, call 0171-638-4141. It is located on the eighth floor of the Barbican Centre (lift and stairs available), Silk Street, EC2.

19

✠✠

London's National Postal Museum

ost first-time visitors to London delight in recognizing the famous landmarks of that great city—Big Ben, the Houses of Parliament, Buckingham Palace, the Tower. But those who return to London again and again look upon arrival for their own favorite, reassuringly familiar totems. Mine is the humble red letter box.

Only of course it is not really so humble. Gracefully crowned at the top and ornamented with the insignia of the reigning sovereign, the freestanding pillar-shaped letter box, emblem of Her Majesty's Royal Mail, can impose an almost regal presence on an otherwise dowdy street. No one would ever refer to such a repository as a mere mail drop. Although letter boxes can be placed in walls (even, as I once saw in Wales, carved into a rock cliff-face), or attached to poles in a form known as a *lamp box*, the venerable pillar box commands the most attention and respect.

How much attention and respect? At the National Postal Museum, located within London's Chief Post Office on King Edward Street near St. Paul's, a visitor can pick up an application to join the Letter Box Study Group. This group, with a current membership of about seven hundred, aims "to accumulate and disseminate information on all aspects of Letter Boxes." Carrying out surveys of rare and historical specimens, the group now maintains a listing of more than three hundred and eighty different models and publishes its notable finds in a quarterly newsletter.

Several such pillar boxes, all slightly different in shape and style, are on display in the lobby of the Chief Post Office. The boxes are cordoned off, perhaps to protect them from unthinking patrons who might try to stuff mail in their antique slots, or perhaps from too-curious visitors who might want to finger the gleaming gold of Queen Victoria's embossed initials. Grouped in a circle, the stately pillar boxes look rather like mysterious standing stones—albeit painted a startling red.

These historical letter boxes are an excellent preamble to the National Postal Museum, just a few steps away. Opened in 1966, yet somehow still undiscovered by most tourists, the well-organized and pleasant museum contains a fascinating set of exhibits. They illuminate not only the history and complexity of the Post Office—an institution whose functions have included a savings bank, telephone and telegraph departments, and many miscellaneous services—but also England itself.

The story of the postal service offers a combination of romance and practicality. An 1828 painting, *The Royal Mail's Departure from the GPO*, by J. Pollard, dramatically illustrates a time when London crowds gathered every night to watch the horse-drawn mail coaches dash off to all parts of the kingdom. (This was never an easy journey. Among museum artifacts is a brass-barreled pistol used by mail-coach guards from 1816 to 1841.) Old photographs show a Welsh postman on horseback, plunging through what looks like waist-high marshland in a determined attempt to deliver the mail; intrepid postmen on bicycles, motorcycles, and in Morris Minor vans; and one rather rakish-looking postman sporting a straw hat, "optional for summer wear."

Mail carriers were not always men. In times of war, women were called to duty. (One of several brief leaflets in the museum describes "Women in the Post Office.") One photograph, available as an unusual postcard in the museum gift shop, illustrates the Corps of Women Drivers and Grooms in World War II. Standing at attention, dressed in double-breasted greatcoats and helmet hats, with coiled long whips in hand, these women exude a fierce pride.

Like any sharply focused museum, the Post Office collection offers unlikely tidbits of information. If I had not grasped the immensity of the Post Office enterprise, among England's largest employers, one picture alone would have convinced me: a corner of the old P. O. clothing store, which stocked at one time tunics in four hundred and fifty sizes, with four sleeve lengths, making eighteen hundred possible fittings. In England's more meticulous days, no postman need have worn too-tight jackets or drooping sleeves. Appearances mattered. Today's Post Office is more suitably represented by a photo of its modern fitness center.

Another display describes Telegram Boys, a grade of service discontinued in the 1970s, a unique class within England's (and the P.O.'s) rigidly structured society. Another leaflet notes: "To maintain smartness and discipline the boys undertook regular drills, section leaders being issued with stripes to wear on their uniforms. The boys had their own rest rooms with a matron looking after their welfare." Though a photograph of the boys was not alarming, I found the idea of regimented Telegram Boys a trifle Dickensian. I read more cheerfully about Smokey, one of the official Post Office cats. Pay and conditions for these cats "were a constant source of debate," according to a placard next to Smokey's picture, since too much food provided meant not enough mice devoured.

After several levels of exhibits about postal history, including a replica of the world's first stamp-canceling machine, a visitor ascends to what must be the inner sanctum for all serious philatelists. In one long room, lined with bronze pull-out files, the Post Office Museum houses and displays the famous Phillips collection of British Victorian stamps; the Public Record collections of the artwork, essays, and registration sheets of all British stamps; and the Universal Postal Union collection of world postage stamps since 1878. Freestanding glass cases hold small acquisitions: postal scales, letter balances, engraving tools, master dies and plates, miniature models of mail vans, and two collections of stamp boxes, made of silver, ormolu, brass, or wood. But the bronze files of stamps hold pride of place.

Walking down the long row of labeled files, which slide silently outward, revealing a thin two-sided glassed cabinet, I felt as if I were studying an abbreviated and rather eccentric compendium of British political, cultural, and social history. One case illustrated the history of the Penny Black, the world's first adhesive postage stamp, issued on May 6, 1840. Another documented Elihu Burritt's one-man campaign for transatlantic penny post in the 1840s and 1850s, a time when England's ambitions stretched around the world.

Next to such sober displays, I found nineteenth-century greeting cards, including elaborate valentines from the 1850s, with even the smallest lavishly engraved: "I think of thee, at midnight hour ..." A whole row of cases was devoted to Dickens, with scenes from his novels commemorated on postcards, all with appropriate quotations. Another surprising case held a set of delicately colored five-by-seven-inch paintings for the centenary of the Royal National Rose Society in 1976—paintings intended, of course, to be magically reduced to stamp size.

As I proceeded to the files of actual stamps, I realized that they might tell anyone who knew nothing about England almost all that was necessary to know. Here was the Commonwealth Collection, reminders of how far the old Empire once stretched: Aden, Antigua, Burma, Ceylon, Fiji, the Falklands, Gibraltar, Ghana, Gold Coast, Guernsey, India, Leeward Islands, Muscat, Norfolk Islands, Pakistan, New Zealand—on and on. Some stamps were unabashedly proud of England's long reach: one labeled Violinist and the Acropolis, picturing a musician in front of the ancient Greek temple, was attributed to the British Council Promoting the Arts. I puzzled awhile about why and what, exactly, the British Council was promoting in Athens. But stamps reveal only so much.

Many of these Commonwealth stamps were astonishingly beautiful. One, showing trekkers in British Antarctic Territory, was a miniature landscape painting, complete with ice sheets, sled dogs, and white mountains in the background. A sailboat on green seas came from the Bahamas, a scrupulously detailed series of gaudy butterflies symbolized Antigua. The very richness of these stamps also evoked the old Empire, a sharp contrast to Britain's current economic straits.

The royal family appeared in almost infinite variations, as ubiquitous in the Commonwealth collection as in Britain's own stamps. Though not individually compelling, the sheer number of these royal portraits provided forceful assurance that despite their recent fall from grace, the Windsors would never be easily expunged. Other stamps also vividly pictured England's particular obsessions. A series on British wildflowers chronicled the Larger Bindweed and Viper's Bugloss with infinitesimal care; another series celebrated village churches such as St. Mary the Virgin, in Huish Episcopi, Somerset. British children's books, still read and treasured by English-speaking children around the world, appeared in a series of illustrations from *The Tale of Peter Rabbit*, *Wind in the Willows*, *Winnie-the-Pooh*, and *Alice's Adventures in Wonderland*. As much attention seemed to have been given to portraits of Toad, Badger, Ratty, and Mole as to the latest profile of Prince Philip—a healthy sign, I thought.

For the serious philatelist, this floor of the museum would offer still more attractions, including copious material on, for instance, the changing image of Britannia; the refinement of stamp-canceling; thousands of original designs, both accepted and unaccepted, for British stamps; and more. Some materials must be requested from storage, but much is on view.

For a less serious visitor, the museum gift shop, located at the entrance/exit, probably has more appeal than a genuine set of proof sheets of the Penny Black. This small shop offers out-of-the-ordinary London souvenirs: a shiny red money tin in the shape of a pillar box, for example, with toffees inside; a polyester tie with stamp designs; red or green pottery banks. One of the handsomest was a black and white silk headscarf bearing an almost abstract design of the Penny Black.

For any mail posted from the museum shop, the Post Office provides its own postmark of a Maltese cross. I stocked up on postcards, including several of the whip-carrying Women

Drivers and Grooms, not to mention a few of an ingenious contraption I hadn't seen in the museum, a bright red five-wheeled cycle, c. 1883, used at Horsham, Sussex, to carry parcels. The high, thin-wheeled, giant-size cycle looked more vintage Victorian than the VR royal initials on those antique pillar boxes.

My most prized postcard, however, is one from the British Postbox Series. In full color, it captures the E II R Type G Pillarbox with Scottish Crown, Type Sheffield 10, a brilliant scarlet letter box pictured against a leafy green street. I don't plan to send it to anybody.

A FEW FLOATING FACTS

Facts do float, and so, in recent months, has the London Chief Post Office. It is now closed, although the National Postal Museum (telephone 0171-239-5420) remains open in the King Edward Building, King Edward Street, London EC1A 1LP, not far from St. Paul's Cathedral. The nearest underground station is at St. Paul's on the Central Line. The museum is open Monday to Friday, nine-thirty A.M. to four-thirty P.M. Admission is free.

20

Bluebell Woods

*T*heir color is almost impossible to describe—a clear, deep azure that mysteriously seems to lighten in sun to shades of violet. On a showery April day, English bluebells glow with vibrant color: the blue of a sky washed clean, bright water in a quiet bay, a nest of robin's eggs, the implicit promise of iris and forget-me-nots. After a dark, cold winter, wild bluebells—actually, wild hyacinths, officially identified either as *endymion nonscriptus* or *scilla nutans*—suddenly appear in astonishing profusion. Certain woodlands, where bluebells thrive in mottled shade, often look as if their spring housekeepers had flung out new bright blue carpets.

Although many Americans in England seek out the drifts of daffodils made so famous by Wordsworth ("I wandered lonely as a cloud ..."), few know exactly where or how to look for bluebells. Daffodils grow easily from bulbs planted almost anywhere, in city parks, squares, and formal gardens. Bluebells, however, are shier and more elusive, a true wildflower clustering in damp areas along woodland paths. Those who want to find bluebells in their full glory must venture beyond London during their brief season of bloom, somewhere from late March into early May. Although a bluebell takes seven years to flower from seed, some woods are so thick with plants that they become known in season as *bluebell woods*.

Fortunately, bluebell woods are seldom far away. Within less than an hour's drive of London, for example, three very different places—a large garden, the small woods belonging to a country house, and the ancient woodland next to a working Sussex farm, all open to the public—have dazzling displays of those delicate bell-shaped flowers. Explorers of the countryside will soon discover other bluebell woods as well.

Bluebells are only one of many attractions at Wakehurst Place Garden, about ten miles southeast of Gatwick Airport. An annex of the Royal Botanic Gardens at Kew, Wakehurst encompasses over five hundred acres, including a walled perennial garden; collections of heather, lilies, and many exotic plants; deep valleys; linked ponds, lake and marshland; a rock walk; and an extensive nature reserve. In April, a visitor who walks through the Himalayan Glade (which displays species that grow at ten thousand feet) will be greeted by early rhododendrons covered with lavish blossoms in white, pink, red, and purple. Under the rhododendrons and along the slopes of the glade, bluebells drift in a soft wash of background color.

On the mid-April morning James and I strolled through Wakehurst, most trees were just beginning to bud. Green seemed to hang in the air like a faint cloud. Cock pheasants wandered everywhere, strutting and screaming. A few hen pheasants, disguised by their duller plumage, hovered nearby in the grass. Ducks and geese swam on the lakes. We walked through the Himalayan Glade and Westwood Valley, then Horsebridge Wood and Bloomer Valley, and back through Bethlehem Wood, a leisurely circuit of about an hour. Wher-

ever we looked, we could see swaths of bluebells, hovering in
the green grass like floating pieces of upside-down sky.

Wakehurst is such a large and varied garden—an American would see it as a landscaped park, with smaller gardens
and floral plantings—that we could have lingered among
bluebells all morning. On sunny days we have often picnicked
on Wakehurst's close-clipped green lawn, which surrounds a
grand mansion of Elizabethan origins. For a quick pick-me-
up, the National Trust provides a self-service tearoom inside
the mansion between Easter and mid-October, but sometimes
we take our cups and saucers outside to bask in the sun and
look out on that astonishingly green carpet of grass, sprinkled
with tiny daisies.

Only a fifteen-minute drive from Wakehurst, we found a
smaller, more intimate bluebell woods at Standen House. A
handsome Victorian home designed by Philip Webb, a friend
of William Morris's, Standen overlooks the Medway Valley.
(See Chapter Fifteen, "Lord of the Manor: Staying at Standen.")
Not many visitors to this National Trust property explore beyond the house itself, with its Morris furnishings and textiles,
and its enchanting, quintessentially English garden. But a few
minutes' walk through a gate and then down a well-marked
path leads to Hollybush Woods.

A deeply sloping tract, Hollybush Woods does not look
large from the outside, but inside, it is surprisingly extensive.
It has an almost secret air, as damp leaf-strewn footpaths with
bridges and stepping stones in wet places dip down into its
green heart. The oak woods, underplanted with hazel and
sweet chestnut, are old and tall, but open enough in spring to
let in a shimmer of sun. In April, the hillsides of Hollybush
Woods are crammed with bluebells, uncountable thousands of

them, mixed with occasional yellow primroses, buttercups, and white anemones.

From the dense green darkness of Hollybush Woods, we returned to the house and took a path leading to an overlook on the steep hillside above it. After admiring the haze-softened view far into the distance, over a reservoir and toward the ancient woods of Ashdown Forest, we followed the path in a brief but lovely loop around the semiwild, shaggier edges of the upper garden. Here, too, we could see small patches of bluebells.

Leaving Standen, we then drove eight miles to Heaven Farm, whose name, we agreed after our visit, seemed just right. With a history traced back to 1387, Heaven Farm is a complex of early nineteenth-century farm buildings, including barn, stables, forge, granary, and oast house. Once a virtually self-sufficient tiny village, it was for centuries the home farm for Danehurst, an adjoining estate. Since 1959 it has been under the guardianship of John Butler, who runs it not only as a farm, but also as a museum, and he arranges educational tours of both the farm and the surrounding Sussex countryside, whose gentle wooded hills, pastoral farmland, rolling downs, and nearby medieval Ashdown Forest have been designated an Area of Outstanding Natural Beauty.

When we pulled into the parking area of Heaven Farm, Mr. Butler was waiting for us, walking stick in hand and two Border collies by his side. A gentle, enthusiastic man who is knowledgeable and articulate about the land and its history, Mr. Butler clearly wants his visitors to share his pride and pleasure in the heritage of Heaven Farm. He volunteered to guide us through the farm trail, a one-and-a-quarter-mile walk through fields and woodlands.

Visitors can also follow a step-by-step brochure, which points out highlights most might otherwise miss, such as an old alder coppice ("wood still used for turnery work, toys, broom-heads and clogs"), a wild pear tree, and rare knee holly, or butchers' broom, said to be once used to clean butchers' chopping blocks.

What most visitors to Heaven Farm in April come for, however, are the bluebell woods. After the legendary hurricane of October 1987, Mr. Butler told us, the woodland was so devastated that his son, who now manages the farm, had decided clearing the damage would be far too expensive. So Mr. Butler decided to make the salvaged woodland pay for itself by opening it to the public. Last year his bluebell woods attracted more than ten thousand people.

Although the farm trail is little more than a mile long, and the wide path is easy to walk, it took us almost two hours. We had to stop frequently to try to absorb the effect of the myriad bluebells that filled the woods. As the light slanted through the trees, waves of flowers turned from blue to blue-green to lavender. Dappled sunlight picked up glints of white anemone and yellow celandine. In this lovingly preserved woodland, the flowers spread so far and so abundantly that they almost seemed an overflowing river of blue, spilling onto the green forest floor.

The bluebell woods have been at Heaven Farm for a long time. Here and there, hidden in the grass, Mr. Butler pointed out bits of charcoal, slag from a Roman *bloomery* for smelting iron. Flecks of white powdery ash were another kind of memorial; some modern visitors are so struck by the serene loveliness of these woods that they ask for their ashes to be scattered there.

Part of the enchantment of these woods was how natural,

yet unobtrusively tended, they were. Mr. Butler has worked hard to keep flora and fauna both alive. During our walk, he took from his jacket pocket a handful of seedlings in small plastic bags, stepped off the path, and quickly pushed them into a few bare spots of earth. On a tiny island in a marshy area, he is trying to create a haven for endangered grass snakes. They need warm compost to lay their eggs, he said, and since his field compost heap does not seem to do the job, he is still searching for the proper combination of ingredients.

Mr. Butler knows each tree and shrub in his woodland, its age, its purpose, and its future. He pointed out silver birch, alder, sweet chestnut, beech, oak (both Turkish and English), ash, hornbeam, and hazel. Since hazel can be used for clothespins, pea and bean sticks, and other handy items, he is hoping to find someone who still has these wood-working skills. Mr. Butler values Sussex crafts and customs. As we passed a gorse bush in flower, he pointed to it and repeated an old Sussex saying: "When the gorse is in bloom, kissing's in season." Fortunately, Mr. Butler added, you can almost always find a flower blooming somewhere on a gorse.

From an old orchard, the trail ran along the edge of open fields. Here Mr. Butler watches after wildflowers, like the pale pink lady smock, white stitchwort, and red wild vetch along a hedge ditch. In the center of a field is a small stand of larch, which he planted simply "because they look so nice." Looking toward the house at Danehurst, we saw a scattering of huge magnificent oaks, as if, Mr. Butler said a well-known gardener had once remarked, "someone had thrown a handful of acorns there."

Back in the farmyard, we settled happily at a table in the sunshine for tea, with a delicious orange chocolate-chip cake prepared by Mr. Butler's daughter, who is in charge of the tea-room, a light and attractive space in the renovated stable. Flamboyant cockerels waddled around the yard, kept (like the stand of larch) for their beauty. Anonymous neighbors some-times drop off unwanted birds at the farm gates, and the Butlers rescue them.

During our walk, Mr. Butler talked about modern agricul-ture in England, the effect of the European Community on policies and pricing, and the difficulty of keeping a place like Heaven Farm going. It is one of the few working farms left in the area. Suddenly he stopped, held up his hand for silence, and called our attention to the sound of a cuckoo not far away. It was the first cuckoo of the spring. He smiled with delight, and so did we.

"You can see why," he said at the end of our tour, "as I look around me on a morning like this, I feel like a wealthy man." As we left the last of our bluebell woods, we felt we had shared the riches of an English spring.

A FEW FLOATING FACTS

Remember to omit the prefix "0" from an English telephone num-ber when calling from the United States. Prices are calculated at $1.60 to the pound.

Wakehurst Place Garden is located one and one-half miles northwest of Ardingly, near Haywards Heath, on the B2028. It can be easily reached by car from London via the (A)M23; the nearest rail station is Haywards Heath, five-and-a-half miles away. Run by the National Trust, Wakehurst is open all year, except Christmas and New Year's Day; in March, ten to six, and in April and May, ten to seven. Admission about £4 ($6.40), reduced rates for students, children, and seniors. Free to members of the National Trust or Royal Oak, its American affiliate.

Standen House, also owned by the National Trust, is two miles south of East Grinstead, West Sussex, signposted from the B2110 (Turners Hill Road). The nearest rail station is East Grinstead, two miles away; by bus take either the 474 London & Country service that runs between East Grinstead and Crawley, getting off at Saint Hill, half a mile from Standen. The house, garden, and woods are open on weekends during March, from twelve-thirty to four-thirty P.M., then from April 1 to October 31, Wednesday to Sunday (also bank holiday Mondays, closed Tuesday following), from twelve-thirty to five-thirty P.M. Admission about £4 ($6.40), reduced rates for students, children, and seniors. Free to members of the National Trust or Royal Oak, its American affiliate. Telephone East Grinstead 01342-323029.

Heaven Farm is near Furners Green, Uckfield, Sussex, easily reached from London via the A22, then the A275 signposted to Lewes and Newhaven. Haywards Heath, seven miles away, is the nearest station. It is six miles from Wakehurst. Open ten to six from Easter to October 31. During bluebell season, it can be crowded on weekends. Admission for adults, £1.90 ($3.04), less for seniors and children. A tearoom serves light snacks; outdoor seating available. Telephone 01825-790226.

It would be possible to take a taxi from Gatwick to Wakehurst in twenty minutes (traffic permitting), to Standen in half an hour, to Heaven Farm in forty-five minutes.

Where to stay: Since all three places are close to Gatwick, hotels, inns, and bed-and-breakfast establishments are plentiful in the area. Perhaps the choicest establishment is Gravetye Manor (near East Grinstead, West Sussex RH19 4LJ), secluded, elegant, *very* expensive, with an excellent restaurant, and set in the midst of its own famous garden designed by William Robinson. Rooms range from £100 ($160), *per room*, with most about £185 ($296), *per room*, not per person, but with VAT added at 17.5 percent. Breakfast not included. Telephone 01342-810567, fax 01342-810080.

The woods at Sliders Farm adjoin Heaven Farm. Sliders Farm (Furners Green, Uckfield, East Sussex TN22 3RT, telephone Danehill 01825-790258) offers bed and breakfast from £25 ($40) per person in a double room, £34 ($54.40) for a single room, reductions for longer stays. Evening meal by request at £14 ($22.40). Three rooms, all with private baths and showers. Tennis court, outdoor (summer) swimming pool, and fishing on the farm's own lakes. A self-catering cottage that sleeps four rents from £275–£400 ($440–$640) weekly, depending on the season.

At Hartfield, a short drive from these three gardens, Stairs Farm House (High Street, Hartfield, East Sussex TN7 4AB, telephone Hartfield 01892-770793) is a modernized house dating from the seventeenth century. It has a tearoom and farm shop. Three rooms, twin/double at £20–21 ($32–33.60) per person, single from £25 ($40) to £32 ($51.20), family room from £15 ($24) to £19 ($30.40) per person. Full English breakfast included.

Planning the Next Trip?

I had been to England more than a dozen times before I first discovered the glories of bluebell woods. I had never before been in the proper place—an undisturbed woodland with just the right balance of sunshine and shadow—at the proper time. Now when I plan a spring visit, I have to decide if I long most to see drifts of daffodils in March, or a carpet of bluebells in April, or rhododendrons ablaze in May. If I'm lucky, I may glimpse all three in some magical garden where climate, location, and unpredictable weather have kept everything blooming.

I mention my discovery of bluebell woods because it is a reminder that innumerable pleasures and surprises still await me, and other fortunate travelers, whenever we return to England. Each time I sit down with my maps, guidebooks, and pad of paper, and begin to make notes for another trip, I realize how much more I have to see and do. When will I walk the Mendip Hills? Explore the Cheddar Gorge? Sail to the Isles of Scilly or the Holy Island of Lindisfarne? Settle quietly for a few days in Alnmouth, a tiny Northumbrian fishing village with clustered red roofs I glimpsed for a moment from our train?

When can I stroll through the garden at Sezincote, which surrounds an English country house built in the Moghul architectural style, complete with an Indian bridge decorated with Brahmin bulls? My current garden listing tells me it is open only on Thursday and Friday afternoons, so I will need to plan carefully. Could James and I go from Sezincote to Peak Cavern in Derbyshire, or perhaps into Shropshire, where we've never stayed? I'd love to stop briefly in Acton Burnell, a village of a few hundred people, whose black and white cottages are, one reference tells me, "as English as they come."

I still have not seen the White Cliffs of Dover, or Cliveden, or Wicken Fen, or Beatrix Potter's Hill Top, or Calke Abbey, or Portmeirion, or Chatsworth, or much of the Midlands, or the Matlocks in Derbyshire, or Lichfield Cathedral—or so many other towns, castles, houses, churches, museums, gardens, and walks.

Perhaps you have now begun to dream about your own next trip to England—whether it is your first or fifteenth— and to make definite plans. Whoever you are, I'd like to picture you slinging your bag over your shoulder as you head for the airport shuttle, or pushing your luggage cart through the door at Gatwick or Heathrow, or setting foot on a dock at Southampton. You glance up at the sky (which will somehow look wonderful, even if gray or misty or downright rainy), take a few breaths of English air, and then pick up your bag, as you eagerly set out to . . . I only hope this book has helped point you in whatever direction you want to go.

Index

A.A. Milne (Thwaite), 178
*AA Inspected Bed and Breakfast in
    Britain,* 35
Abbotsbury Gardens, Dorset, 127
Abbotsbury Swannery, Dorset,
    12, 127
Acton Burnell, Shropshire, 233
Adams, Henry, 159
Aga, 30
Aira Force, Lake District, 15
Air travel, 61–66
Alnmouth, Northumbria, 232
Amazon (yacht), 49–50
Anglesey, 55
Ardclach Bell Tower, Scotland,
    149
Arlington Court, Devon, 196
Arundel, Sussex, 34
Ashdown Forest, Sussex, 168-178,
    226
Ashdown Forest (Christian), 170
Ashdown Forest Farm, Sussex,
    175-176
Aultbea, Scotland, 137

Austen, Jane, 127
Automobilia, Cornwall, 111
Ayrton, Michael, 208
A-Z maps, 58–59

Badachro, Scotland, 135
Balmoral Castle, Scotland, 134
Barber and Surgeons Hall
    Gardens, London, 213
Barbican, London, 204, 205, 213
Barbican Conservatory, London,
    213–215
Barkham Manor Vineyard,
    Sussex, 176
Bar Lodge, Cornwall, 114–115,
    120
Barnstable, Devon, 196
Barrington Court, Dorset, 124
Bath Hotel, Lynmouth, Devon,
    197
Bathrooms, 28–29, 35
Beaminster, Dorset, 122, 131
Bed-and-breakfasts (B&Bs), 13,
    32, 35–36

Bede, 170

Bedgebury Pinetum, Kent, 15, 90–91

Beinn Eighe, Scotland, 138–139

Best Bed and Breakfast in the World, The, 35

Betjeman, Sir John, 12, 23

Billingsgate Market, London, 211

Biscuits, 78–79

Black Isle, Scotland, 144

Blackmore, R. D., 16, 194

Blake, William, 205

Bluebell Railway, Sussex, 176

Bluebell woods, 223–232

Bodmin Moor, Cornwall, 111, 113

Border country, 133

Breakfast, 34, 36, 68, 70

Brendon, Devon, 194

Brendon Common, Devon, 194

Bridge House Hotel, Beaminster, Dorset, 131

Bridport, Dorset, 130

Bristol Channel, 193, 194

British Tourist Authority, 14, 26, 51, 142, 152

BritRail's British Travel Bookshop, Ltd., 14, 51–52, 59

Broadgate Development, London, 207

Broads, 55

Broadstone Trail, Sussex, 171

Brodie Castle, Scotland, 151

Brympton d'Evercy, Dorset, 125

Buckland Abbey, Devon, 93

Bude, Cornwall, 157

Bungalows, 35

Bunhill Fields Graveyard Garden, London, 205–206, 215

Bunyan, John, 205

Burghead Bay, Scotland, 147–148

Burritt, Elihu, 219

Butler, John, 226–229

Cadhay Manor, Dorset, 130

Calke Abbey, 233

Camel Trail, Cornwall, 15

Candy, 79

Canterbury Cathedral, Kent, 129

Car boot sales, 45

Carclew Gardens, Cornwall, 46–47, 94, 117–118

Carrick Roads, Cornwall, 117

Carry-on bag, 62–63

Car travel, 17–18, 39–42

Castles
  in Cornwall, 159–167
  in Scotland, 149–151

Castle Stuart, Scotland, 151

Catalogues, 27–30

Cave of Gold, Scotland, 143

Cawdor, Lord, 150–151

Cawdor Castle, Scotland, 149–151

Central heating, 29

Cerne Abbas, Dorset, 126–127

Chadwick, Steve, 142–143

Chard, Dorset, 124

Charlie, Bonnie Prince, 152, 199

Chatsworth, Derbyshire, 233

Cheddar Gorge, Somerset, 232

Chedington, Dorset, 121–122, 130–131

Chedington Court, Dorset, 130–131

Chesil Beach, Dorset, 59

Christian, Garth, 170

Churchill, Winston, 210

Clapton Court, Dorset, 12, 125

Clava Cairns, Scotland, 146

Cleary Gardens, London, 209–210

Cleeve Abbey, Devon, 196

Cliff Railway, Lynmouth, Devon, 192–193

Cliveden House, Buckinghamshire, 233

Cloth Fair flat, London, 92

Clothing, 73–76

Coach travel, 61–66

Coffee mornings, 45, 104

Coleridge, Samuel Taylor, 16

Compton House, Dorset, 128

Computer, 87

Condell, Henry, 210

Conrad, Joseph, 114

Consumer Reports' The Bed and Breakfast Guide to Great Britain, 35

Consumer Reports Travel Letter, 19, 32, 41, 52

Continental breakfast, 34

Cookies, 78–79

Cornish Gardens Trust, 46

Cornwall, 4–5, 16, 24, 43, 46–47, 59, 93, 96, 99–120, 157, 159–167

Cotehele House, Cornwall, 43

Cottages (*see* Holiday flats and cottages)

Countisbury Hill, Devon, 195

Countryside Commission's National Trail Guides, 48

Crackers, 78–79

Crewkerne, Dorset, 125

Cricket St. Thomas Wildlife Park, Dorset, 89–90, 129

Cromwell, Oliver, 164, 205

Cromwell, Thomas, 212

Crumpets, 80

Culbin Forest, Scotland, 145

Culbin Sands, Scotland, 145

Culbone Church, Devon, 196

Culloden, battle of, 48, 199–200

Culloden House Hotel, Inverness, Scotland, 152

DairyLand Farm World, Cornwall, 111

Danehurst, Sussex, 175, 226, 228

Daphne Du Maurier (Forster), 120

Dartmoor, Devon, 55, 113, 128

Defoe, Daniel, 205

De La Warr, Earl, 169

Derbyshire, 55, 233

Devices and Desires (James), 17

Devon, 4, 24, 55, 87, 93, 113, 128, 157, 189–197

Devon Coastal Path, 191

Dickens, Charles, 220

Discount programs, 32–33, 52–53

Distances, 18

Diston's Cottage, Cotswolds, 24

Doone Country, 16, 194

Dorset, 12, 59, 89–90, 121–131

Dorset Coastal Path, 127–128

Driving, 39–40

Drumnadrochit, Scotland, 13–14

Drumossie Moor, Scotland, 152, 200, 203

Du Maurier, Daphne, 16, 110–120

Dunster Castle, Devon, 196

East Grinstead, Sussex, 179, 230

East Lambrook Manor, Dorset, 12, 126

East Lyn River, Devon, 195

Eating (*see* Meals)

Eden Court Theatre, Inverness, Scotland, 48–49

Edinburgh, Scotland, 133

Edward II, King of England, 169

Ehrlich, George, 209

Enchanted Cornwall (Du Maurier), 110, 120

Enchanted Places, The (C. Milne), 172, 173, 177

English Tourist Board, 35, 52

En suite, 29

Entertainment Halfprice Europe, 53

Evershot, Dorset, 126

Exmoor, Somerset, 16, 55, 113, 157, 189, 192, 194, 195

Exmoor National Park Information Centre, 197

Fairy Loch, Scotland, 201–203

Farmhouse B&Bs, 36

Fast food restaurants, 38

Festival Gardens, London, 209

Findhorn, Scotland, 12, 147

Findhorn Foundation, 147

Findhorn River, Scotland, 148–149

Finsbury Circus, London, 207–208

Finsbury Square, London, 206

First-class travel, 62–66

Fish, Marjorie, 126

Flambards Village Theme Park, Cornwall, 110

Fo'c'sle Cottage, Padstow, Cornwall, 100, 109

Food (*see* Meals)

Forde Abbey, Dorset, 124

Forres, Scotland, 148

Forster, Margaret, 119, 120

Fortune Street Garden, London, 205, 206

Fowles, John, 127

Fraser, Simon, 212

French Lieutenant's Woman, The (Fowles), 127

Frenchman's Creek, Cornwall, 115–116

Frenchman's Creek (Du Maurier), 110, 114, 116

From Nairn to Loch Ness (Meldrum), 146

Furners Green, Sussex, 230, 231

Gairloch, Scotland, 133–143, 201

Gardens, 16, 59, 85

in Cornwall, 105–108, 117–118, 166
in Devon, 196
in Dorset, 123–127
guides to, 43–44, 106, 107, 204, 213
in London, 204–215
in Scotland, 135–136
in Sussex, 182, 186, 224–230
Gardens of England & Wales, 44
Gatwick Airport, 230
Geographers' A-Z, 58, 60
Gills Lap, Sussex, 174, 175
Glasgow, Scotland, 133
Glassenbury Park, 44–45
Glastonbury, Somerset, 16
Glastonbury Abbey, Somerset, 59, 165
Glencoe, Scotland, 55, 199
Glen Lyn Estate, Devon, 194–195
Golden Cap, Dorset, 128
Golf View Hotel, Nairn, Scotland, 152–153
Good Food Guide, The, 37
Good Gardens Guide, The, 43, 106, 107, 204, 213
Gravetye Manor, East Grinstead, Sussex, 231
Great Cornish Holiday Trail, 110
Great Dixter, Sussex, 59
Great Wapses Farm, Henfield, Sussex, 36
Greyfriars Garden, London, 210
Grocers, 38–39
Gypsies, 91

Hardy, Thomas, 122
Hardy's Cottage, Dorset, 130
Hartfield, Sussex, 168, 171, 231
Hawk Conservancy, Hampshire, 15
Haywards Heath, Sussex, 229, 230
Heale House, Wiltshire, 85, 88
Heating, 29
Heaven Farm, Sussex, 175, 226–230
Heddon's Mouth, Devon, 194
Helston, Cornwall, 111–112
Heminge, John, 210
Herriot, James, 16
Highlands of Scotland, 133–153, 199–203
Hill Top, Cumbria, 233
Historic Houses, Castles & Gardens, 130
Hoar Oak Water, Devon, 195
Hobhouse, Penelope, 129
Holiday flats and cottages, 12, 13, 100, 109, 114–115, 120, 135, 142, 144, 152, 183, 184, 187, 196, 197
Hollybush farmhouse, Sussex, 186
Hollybush Woods, Sussex, 225–226
Holy Island of Lindisfarne, 232
Holywell, Dorset, 126
Hotels, 31–34, 121–122, 130–131, 139–140, 151–153, 191, 196–197, 231
House at Pooh Corner, The (Milne), 168
Hunter's Hatch, South Perrott, 131

Ilminster, Dorset, 124
Inverewe, Scotland, 135–136
Inverness, Scotland, 48, 147, 199
Isle of Skye, 133, 134, 137, 141
Isles of Scilly, 232

Jack the Giant Killer legend, 163
Jamaica Inn, Cornwall, 113
Jamaica Inn (Du Maurier), 110, 111, 113, 114
James, P. D., 17
Jams and jellies, 80
Jekyll, Gertrude, 124
Jenny Wren's, Beaminster, Dorset, 131
Jewett, Sarah Orne, 114
John of Gaunt, Duke of Lancaster, 169
Johnstone, George, 107
Journal, 86–94
Jumble (rummage) sales, 45, 104

Kent, 15, 43, 59, 88, 90–91, 129, 157, 169, 171
Kitchens, 30–31
Kynance Cove, Cornwall, 119

Lake District, 15, 16, 55, 157
Landmark Trust, 22–25, 52, 92
Landranger Map, 56–57, 142, 148, 174
Lanhydrock, Cornwall, 106–108
Lehman Brothers, 207
Lettaford Chapel, Devon, 24

Lichfield Cathedral, Staffordshire, 233
Lizard Point, Cornwall, 119
Loch Braigh Horrisdale, Scotland, 201–202
Loch Ewe, Scotland, 136
Loch Gairloch, Scotland, 135, 137, 201
Loch Lomond, Scotland, 55
Loch Maree, Scotland, 136, 138–139
Loch Maree Hotel, Scotland, 139–140
Loch Ness, Scotland, 49, 50
Lodging
   bed-and-breakfasts (B&Bs), 13, 32, 35–36
   catalogues, 27–30
   holiday flats and cottages, 12, 13, 100, 109, 114–115, 120, 135, 142, 144, 152, 183, 184, 187, 196, 197
   hotels, 31–34, 121–122, 130–131, 139–140, 151–153, 191, 196–197, 231
   rental agencies, 19–22
   renting from owners, 25–27
   trust properties, 21–25
Loe Pool, Cornwall, 115–117
London
   gardens in, 204–215
   National Postal Museum, 216–222
London Sunday Times, 21, 25
London Wall Walk, 212–213
Long Man, 59

Lowe, Stephen, 49–50
Lowlands, 133
Luggage, 5, 72–76
Lyme Regis, Dorset, 127
Lyndale House, Lynmouth,
    Devon, 196
Lynmouth, Devon, 4, 189–197
Lynton, Devon, 87, 189, 193, 197

Macbeth (Shakespeare), 150–151
Magazine advertisements, 19, 21
Makepeace, John, 122, 123
Malmsmead, Devon, 194
Manor House, Beaminster,
    Dorset, 131
Mapperton House, Dorset,
    123–124
Maps, 14–15, 54–60, 142
Marazion, Cornwall, 159, 167
Marmalades, 80
Martinhoe, Devon, 194
Marwood Hill, Devon, 196
Matlocks, Derbyshire, 233
Meals
    breakfast, 34, 36, 68, 70
    eating in, 68–71
    eating out, 37–39, 67–69,
        152–153
    fast food restaurants, 38
    pub, 38, 90
Medway Valley, 182, 225
Meldrum, Edward, 146
Menabilly, Cornwall, 117
Mendip Hills, Somerset, 232
Milne, A. A., 168, 171–175, 178
Milne, Christopher, 172, 173, 177

Milton Abbey, Dorset, 130
Minehead, Devon, 196
Minterne, Dorset, 126–127
Montacute House, Dorset,
    125–126
Mont St. Michel, France, 159, 160
Mont St. Michel and Chartres
    (Adams), 159
Moray Firth, Scotland, 133, 144,
    145
More, Sir Thomas, 212
Morris, William, 182, 184, 185,
    225
Motoring Atlas, 55
M roads, 18, 109
Museum of Mechanical Music,
    Goldsithney, Cornwall, 59
*My Love Affair with England: A
    Traveler's Memoir* (Toth), 3,
    6, 9, 99

Nairn, Scotland, 133, 144–146,
    152–153
National Gardens Scheme, 44, 45,
    117
National Postal Museum,
    London, 216–222
National Trust, 21–25, 43, 52,
    105, 106, 108, 120, 124, 160,
    167, 179, 187, 225, 229, 230
Nevis, 55
New Forest, Hampshire, 55
New Lodge, Trelissick,
    Cornwall, 24
New York Times, 19
Nicolson, Nigel, 169

Nigel Nicholson's Kent, 169
Norfolk, 17, 157
North Downs, 170
North Walk, Lynmouth, Devon, 193
North York Moors, 55

Oare, Devon, 16
Old Mill Cottage, Severn Valley, 24
Old Soar Manor, Plaxtol, Kent, 88
Omelettes, 37
Opinan, Scotland, 143
Ordnance Survey maps, 5, 14, 48, 53–60, 142
Ottery St. Mary, Dorset, 130
Outdoor Leisure Map, 57, 58
Owl House Gardens, Kent, 59
Owners, renting from, 25–27

Packing, 5, 72–76
Padstow, Cornwall, 99–103, 109
Parnham House, Dorset, 122–123
Pathfinder Map, 57–58, 112
Peak Cavern, Derbyshire, 233
Peak District, Derbyshire, 55
Pencarrow, Cornwall, 105–106
Penrose Estate, Cornwall, 115
Penzance, Cornwall, 159, 162
Pets, souvenirs for, 81
Photographs, 89–90
Pilsdon Pen, Dorset, 128
Piltdown Man, 176
Planning, 9–53
    discount programs, 32–33, 52–53

eating (*see* Meals)
itinerary, 15–17
lodging (*see* Lodging)
maps, 14–15, 54–60
on-the-spot, 42–45
packing, 72–76
rental cars, 39–42
time, 17–19
Tourist Information Centres, 47–48
Polgwynne, Cornwall, 117
Pollard, J., 217
Pooh Corner, Hartfield, Sussex, 168, 171–173
Poohsticks Bridge, Hartfield, Sussex, 173–174
Poolewe, Scotland, 135
Poolewe to Gruinard, Selected Walks and Caves (Chadwick), 142
Porlock Harbor, Devon, 195
Porthleven, Cornwall, 93, 114, 119
Portmeirion, 233
Posingford Wood, Sussex, 173
Postman's Park, London, 208–209, 215
Potter, Beatrix, 16, 233
Prideaux Place, Cornwall, 103
Pubs, 38, 90
Puffin Island, 103
Purton Green, Suffolk, 24

Raleigh, Sir Walter, 100
Randolph's Leap, Scotland, 149
Reading, on airplanes, 64

Rebecca (Du Maurier), 110, 112, 114, 117

Redpoint, Scotland, 140

Reed Information Services, 130

Rental agencies, 19–22

Rental cars, 39–42

Rental cottages (*see* Holiday flats and cottages)

Restaurants, 37, 38, 67–71

Ribbentrop, Joachim von, 165

Ridley, Michael, 172

Rising Sun Inn, Lynmouth, Devon, 191, 197

River Heddon, Devon, 194

Riverside Walkway, London, 211

Road Atlas, 14, 55

Road signs, 40

Robert Fleming Holdings Ltd., 27

Robinson, William, 231

Rodmell, East Sussex, 43

Room service, 69

Rossetti, Dante Gabriel, 185

Round-abouts, 39–40

Round House, Nairn, Scotland, 144, 152

Routemaster, 55

Routeplanner, 55

Royal Botanic Gardens, Kew, 224

Royal Mail's Departure from the GPO, The (Pollard), 217

Royal Oak Foundation, 43, 52, 230

Rudland & Stubbs, London, 209

St. Agnes Leisure Park, Cornwall, 110

St. Alphage Garden, London, 213, 215

St. Anne and St. Agnes Garden, London, 210, 215

St. Aubyn family, 160–162, 164

St. Bartholomew the Great, London, 92

St. Dunstan's Church Garden, London, 210–211

St. George's Vineyard, Sussex, 176

St. Mary Aldermanbury Garden, London, 210, 215

St. Mary Staining Garden, London, 210

St. Merryn, Cornwall, 104

St. Michael's Mount, Cornwall, 4–5, 43, 159–167

St. Paul's Cathedral, London, 92, 204, 209, 215, 222

Salads, 37

Salisbury Cathedral, 84, 88, 129

Sandwiches, 38

Sandymouth Bay, Cornwall, 157

Scotland, 132–153, 198–203

Scotland Self-Catering, 26, 142, 152

Scottish National Tourist Board, 26, 142, 152

Seal Sanctuary, Gweeki, Cornwall, 118–119

Seatown, Dorset, 127

Self-catering, 19–31, 71 (*see* also Holiday flats and cottages)

Selworthy Green, Devon, 196

Sezincote Garden, Gloucestershire, 232–233

Shakespeare, William, 150, 210

Sheffield Park Garden, Sussex, 176

Shelley's Cottage, Lynmouth, Devon, 197

Shepard, E. H., 169, 171, 174, 177

Sherborne Abbey, Dorset, 129

Sherborne Castle, Dorset, 130

Short Walks Around Gairloch (Chadwick), 142

Shropshire, 233

Sidmouth, Dorset, 12, 129–130

Sissinghurst Castle, Kent, 43, 59

Sliders Farm, Furners Green, Sussex, 231

Slioch, Scotland, 139, 201

Snowdonia, 55

Soups, 79–80

South Downs, 157, 175

South Petherton, Dorset, 126

Southwest Coast: Padstow to Falmouth, 48

South West Peninsula Coastal Path, 193–194

Souvenirs, 77–83, 221

Spanish Armada, 165

Spread Eagle Inn, Stourhead, Wiltshire, 85, 88

Stafford, Thomas Wentworth, Earl of, 212

Stairs Farm House, Hartfield, Sussex, 231

Standen House, Sussex, 43, 93, 179–188, 225, 230

Stewart, Carl, 20

Stonehenge, 59, 84–85, 88

Stourhead, Wiltshire, 85, 88

Stourhead Garden, Wiltshire, 43

Sueno's Stone, Scotland, 148

Supermarkets, 77–83

Sussex, 34, 36, 43, 59, 93, 157, 168–188, 224–231, 225

Swiss Cottage, Endsleigh, Devon, 24

Taste of Scotland, 153

Telephones, 51

Telford, Thomas, 144

Tess of the D'Urbervilles (Hardy), 122

Thumbprint theory of travel, 97–98

Thwaite, Ann, 171, 178

Tintinhull Garden, Dorset, 129

Toiletries, 81–82

Tors Hotel, Lynmouth, Devon, 191, 196

Tourist Information Centres, 47–48

Tourist Map, 55–56, 58

Tower of London, 212

Travel guides, 13

Travel journal, 86–94

Trebah Garden, Cornwall, 118

Trerice, Cornwall, 107–109

Trevose Head, Cornwall, 104

Trinity Square, London, 211–212

Triton Court, London, 206–207, 209

Trossachs, Scotland, 55

Trust properties, 21–25

Twewithen Gardens, Cornwall, 107

Uckfield, Sussex, 230, 231

Valley of the Rocks, Lynton, Devon, 193
Vanishing Cornwall (Du Maurier), 110, 120
VAT (Value Added Tax), 34
Vegetarian Guide to the Scottish Highlands and Islands, The, 48
Victoria, Queen of England, 134, 139, 141
Village fetes, 45

Wakehurst Place Gardens, Sussex, 43, 224–225, 229–230
Walks Around and About Nairn, 146
Walks Around Crewkerne, 48
Walks for Motorists, 47
Walks from Your Car, 47
Walks in Wester Ross (Welsh), 142
Water bottle, 63
Watersmeet, Devon, 195
Watts, Isaac, 205
Weald, 169
Webb, Philip, 182, 184, 185, 225
Welsh, Mary, 142

Welsh Walks and Legends: South Wales, 48
West Lyn River, Devon, 194, 195
Where to Stay: Farmhouses, Bed & Breakfast Inns and Hostels, 35
White Cliffs of Dover, 233
White Cockade Society, 48, 199–200
Wicken Fen, 233
Wilderness Wood, Sussex, 176–177
Wind Whistle Pub, Dorset, 90
Winnie-the-Pooh (Milne), 168
Winyard's Gap Inn, Chedington, Dorset, 131
Woodland Walks in South-West England, 47
Woolf, Virginia, 114
Wordsworth, William, 16, 223
World of Model Railways, Cornwall, 111
Worldwide Butterflies and Lullingstone Silk Farm, Dorset, 128–129
Wren, Christopher, 210, 211
Wyatt, Sir Thomas, 212

Yeovil, Dorset, 125
Yorkshire, 16, 157

Sean Fitzgerald

ABOUT THE AUTHOR

SUSAN ALLEN TOTH is an adjunct professor of English at Macalester College and a writer whose work has appeared in *The New York Times*, *The Washington Post*, *Harper's*, *Victoria*, *Vogue*, *Travel and Leisure*, *McCall's*, and other newspapers and magazines. Her previous books are *Blooming*, *Ivy Days*, *How to Prepare for Your High-School Reunion*, and *My Love Affair with England*. She lives in Minneapolis with her husband James Stageberg.